Translated by Anne Collier and Christel Petermann
ISBN 3-89268-031-0

UnmentionableS

THE ALLURE OF LINGERIE

by Claire Paillochet

TACO

It is sometimes made of silk, settling like a precious whisper in the hollow part of the hip. Or of lace, holding in its detailed netting the tender weight of a breast. Or of satin, coolly caressing a stomach, or of cosy cotton flannel, fluffy and provincial, best for keeping chilly schoolgirls warm. Under the little seductive flounces, corset-bones or restraining braces are often discovered playing unexpected yet welcome roles. In nylon it sheathes, in dotted swiss it coyly declares not guilty, and in lambskin it damns; in a pliant danskin of pale flesh color or perhaps indecisive beige, it boldly upholds the excesses of nature's generosity. In pure, combed cotton it allows big girls' bottoms to maintain the innocence of childhood. Sadomasochists, meanwhile, prefer it in leather, consistent with their consensual perversity, or in shiny latex, polished nylon, or wonderfully flexible rubber. Laced, zipped, or buckled, but always black. Imagine a cruel woman, heels spiked and whip swinging—she could never be harnessed in candy pink or baby blue. It would cause uncontrollable laughter and a confused collapse of the senses. No, sadomasochists feel like themselves only in absolute black, satanic and sulfurous. Colors are for others, those who love it without wickedness, but not without passion. Colors are for those who dream of stroking, caressing, sublimating, and rumpling it, or of holding it close as a remembrance, but also of dirtying it with ecstasies during nights of sweet sleeplessness. It gracefully allows itself to be maneuvered, conscious nevertheless of its great power, because it is everywhere: on the bodies of women and in the minds of men. After a brief eclipse, it has again taken the upper hand . . . But, after all, what exactly is it? "It," is IT, of course. The garter belt, the boustier, the corset, the dressing gown, the stocking, the panty, the corselet, the body suit, the g-string, the string bikini, the bra, the teddy, the waist-cincher, the half slip, the negligee, tap pants, pantaloons, everything that is worn underneath; protecting delicate skins from direct contact with the rough fabrics which are worn over, and, above all, driving men absolutely insane.

It is only lingerie that conjures so many delightful fantasies. Panties. The girdle. The stocking suspender and its direct rival, the leg garter. The nighties. The camisole. The slip. The fitted corselet. They are the intermediate stages between being completely naked or completely dressed. It is the magic moment when desire must face one last obstacle, made of lace and promises. Some women wear a little garter belt just under their skirt, discreet but wickedly exciting, spicing up (without excess) their everyday dress. Others have adopted the whole panoply, a provocative, black fitted corselet, silk stockings, and little panties slit right where they should be. Or rather where they shouldn't be. It depends on the point of view one adopts: that of the Church or that of the sinner . . . The use of decorative underwear dates back to the beginning of time. Mrs. Cro-Magnon wore a tempting leg garter made of bison to seduce her husband . . . no? Well then, maybe it doesn't go back that far, after all. But by the time the gods of Olympus held sway, even though the Greeks lived naked under their short tunics and knew not of underclothes, women wrapped fine thin sashes around their hips and under their bosoms as a matter of style. This avant-garde underwear had no function other than to draw gentlemen's attention to those particularly attractive zones of the feminine anatomy. The more modern leg garter serves the same purpose, encircling an erotic part of the body. And it is not surprising that Roman women, who had not the faintest idea of what a stocking was, invented the original leg garter, only because it looked pretty above the knee . . . If the leg garter could be considered the ancestor of naughty underwear, then the corset would be more of a prehistoric monster: heavy, idiotic and cumbersome as a dinosaur, incapable of surviving the slightest evolution. Even so, when a mail-order catalog is opened to the "full-figured women" section, it is easy enough to realize that, with underwear, the tertiary era is still with us. The experienced eye will easily recognize the modern derivatives of the 19th century corset in today's full-length girdle. which is usually made of stiffened brassiere cups with smaller reinforcing bones, and double airtight panels. Looking at these photos, one cannot help but feel that these fortresses are invulnerable. And is there really a woman inside?

In the history of sexy underwear, it has been very rough going for men at times, with a particularly awful stage coming towards the end of the Sixties. Coming from God knows where, word got around that naughty underwear had a dual objective—to infringe upon the cherished liberty of women, and to set aflame the basest instincts of men. Filled with horror and violence, women with feminist tendencies sold off or mercilessly burned anything resembling lingerie. It was the great massacre of innocent underthings. Garlands of ill-fated bras, which had nothing sexy about them save for their function, were publicly set afire in vast "happenings" that bordered on sacrificial rituals. Freed at last from 2000 years of Judeo-Christian constraint, feminists embarked, chests to the wind, toward a better future. They barely had time to ruin a scant few brassiere manufacturers when the most formidably endowed among them observed with horror the undeniable traces of collapse in the area of their decolletage. Gulp! Their breasts were sagging, and with them, their morale. They were forced to admit that a fragile bosom has never held the pretense of supporting itself all alone, and that there was indeed value in the corset-bone. In short, a return to the bra, reinforced on either side due to the premature aging of the delicate tissues. They purchased matching panties for aesthetic equilibrium, and suddenly realized that not only sadists went crazy over intimate little flounces. The proof? Their own boyfriends, nice, healthy and clean, had begun to tire of love without veils, of direct sex on all channels. Charms with no mystery soon exhaust their possibilities, and after a while, love seemed like eating in a fast food restaurant—undressed and quickly dressed again, nourished but only partially sated. Even the most acrobatic lovers began to show worrisome signs of weakness, combined with a growing disinterest in the act itself. Some averted the problem by changing partners daily, to enjoy the fleeting and frustrating pleasure, every night, of sliding a banal piece of clothing down thighs whose principal attraction was being unknown.

Most women, however, were not wildly enthusiastic about the idea of being used in the vulgar, disposable manner more typical of facial tissue. This war of satin and lace made things nicer for at least two sec tors of society: underwear tossed to the weeds by feminists was salvaged by gentlemen far more feminine than they, who used it to stimulate their ambiguous sexualities, and ladies of the evening quintupled their business revenues by seducing those men who were nostalgic for hidden frou-frou. All things considered, the pieces were falling into place: women without underwear began asking themselves questions, while men sighed in front of fine linger ie store windows. If a television ser ial were invented called "The Great Remakes of History," sexy under garments would certainly be given a starring role. And this really is a glamorous comeback, rather than a new and modern form, or the free adaptation of a genius scheme born of an inspired designer's unbridled imagination. It is visceral ly "retro" and necessarily passé: no one would consider inventing a revolutionary and futurist design for underwear, made of bizarre fabric and strange in shape, recalling nothing in the memories of men, re minding them of nothing, making no allusions to yesteryear. Because that would be too much, the opposite of the desired effect. What gentlemen are awaiting, with all the strength of a long-frustrated desire, is a return to the underwear of yore, corresponding to a perfectly established code, familiar as a fox hunt. When they give free reign to their fantasies, they envelop a woman's body in giftwrapping covered with little bows, in paper made of silk, crumpling under the fingers, rustling and full of discoveries, with instructions for use on the box. Go ahead, men, it's Christmas . . . Of course, the taste for underwear is paradoxical. In order to simplify the relationship with a lover's body, Man complicates it. . . One may ask all the questions one wants. Why is there this need to exacerbate yet constrain desire, why seek out the special effect or the detailed artifice, when it would be so much simpler to bite right into the naked body? Desire is ambiguous, facetious, unstable. Not always easy to identify, but always impossible to lock up in dogma. It is woven from a fabric of clashes and contradictions, inconsistent, and not even loyal to itself.

As for those who would ask: why want a woman who remains dressed, who removes very little clothing, or takes it off at the last moment possible, forcing one to follow a veritable trail of lace and ribbon, when all you want is to talk body to body, the underwear amateur will answer: why go into a store to buy a very complicated box of games and, once back home, go crazy trying to figure out the rules, when you could just as well play "Old Maid" or solitaire forever, or better yet, play nothing at all, but just sit for hours on your bed staring out the window, watching the day begin and end? As soon as there is action there is complication. The return of underwear is not an ingenious plan, and at the same time it is one. Because it is not the manufacturers, the designers, the creators of style, accustomed to deciding for women what they will wear, who have chosen to bring back the garter belt. No, this time it is the lovers who have imposed their point of view. This means that when a man really wants something, he figures out a way to get it. It also means that it is not a question of an artificial and transient style. Of course, women are not going to change all their habits overnight. Of course, they are not all going to sacrifice themselves to the cult of fishnet stockings and fitted corselets. There will always be the stubborn ones, and there will always be times when nothing can take the place of a good old beat-up pair of jeans. But underwear is out to reconquer the feminine market, and anyone who can hinder it is cunning indeed. Or rather, very idiotic . . . Full of evil intentions, men bring their lovelies into lingerie shops and exhibit infinite patience advising them. The ladies try on little nighties trimmed with maribou feathers, little body suits of silk and lace, equipped with stocking suspenders, flowing pantaloons slit high up the side, and wicked, tightly fitted corselets which inflate the bosom. Oblivious to the pink-saturated decor, in which everything seems more fragile, precious and intimate, they stand where they are least in the way, between a stiff pedestal table and a pile of flat boxes ready to topple over, attentive and serious about the pleasure they are soon to offer themselves . . .

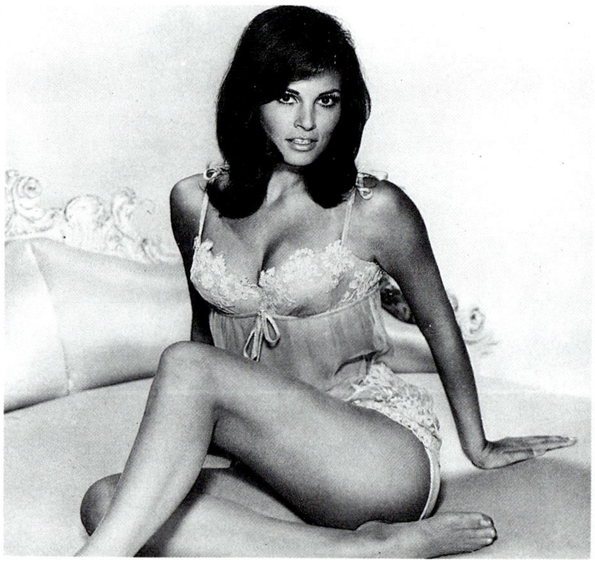

Underwear of this caliber having charmed them with its luxurious caressing of their tender curves, women take the initiative and prepare for what comes next. Addicted to the gradual sliding of silk, they try on all the styles in stock and buy those which especially flatter their feminine forms. For those who revel in lace, it is the end of the practical era, of clothing reduced to its simplest function: supporting and protecting. Women who understand the numerous advantages of seductive clothing feel that this era deprived them of an inexhaustible source of satisfaction. But it would be simplistic to imagine that underwear has reclaimed the same place it had in Grandpa's good old days, to think that the same items are being bought, picking up as though nothing had happened. On the contrary, today's underclothing has a completely different context from that of yesterday. It has lost its primary function, which was a stage in dressing, a hidden aspect of womanhood, and has become an outfit unto itself, a piece of clothing made primarily to be seen. A woman in underwear is not necessarily waiting to put on a dress. She is already dressed, and hopes to unleash precise reactions from men. It is a state of premeditated provocation, and whatever happens to her next, she has carefully cultivated. And she deserves whatever she gets.

Thirty years ago, when a woman wore seamed stockings and a garter belt, it was not necessarily a matter of choice. All of her friends, as well as her mother and all the other women she came across in the street, wore the same undercover accoutrements. Suggestive underwear was inherent to her status as a woman. It was just as natural for her to attach a stocking to a garter as it was to tease her hair. The girl who makes the same gesture today is more conscious of the choice implied; others may wear pants or tights, but she has chosen to affect a garter. She feels her waistline being hugged high up, and the elastic stretching tightly against the naked skin of her thighs. She thinks of it when she walks, when she sits down. Her gestures lose all innocence, because she is conscious of the slightest tension against her skin. When she looks at a man, her uneasiness shows in her eyes and, if he is not completely mentally deficient, he understands immediately that confronting him is a wise woman ripe with the possibility that she is the wearer of secret underclothing!

THE UNDERWEAR AFFAIR

Undies open and bottoms up

Lavish, frilled underwear that drives men to dream is only one century old. Light, easily washable underwear, sometimes resembling a big shirt, was worn by women from the days of antiquity, creating a protective layer underneath. Then, towards the 12th and 17th centuries, there came the monied "rich styles," wherein outer as well as under layers leaned towards the complex and the copious. But fashion was still at the level of piles of petticoats and tunics. There were still no specially designed articles of clothing to hide the more provocative parts of the body; the breasts, for example, were supported simply by the tautly stretched fabric of a shirt tucked into a light corset. Men did not complain about these minimalist undergarments, especially when women fell from their horses, head over heels and, stunned by their fall, lay half naked on the ground until help arrived. It also simplified making love on the sly, since one could simply rearrange the dress and petticoats at a moment's notice and adopt an innocent air to fool any bystanders. None of the cumbersome outfits invented to separate the first layer of fabric from a woman's body, known at the time as a pannier, hoop, bustle, farthingale or crinoline, could fend off the furtive embraces.

Things became more complicated during the mid 19th century and, beginning in 1880, women were literally prisoners of their underwear! They wore not only a long shirt but also a gigantic corset compressing them from the shoulders to the thighs, and to top it all off, an under-bodice, bloomers, and several slips, not to mention leg garters backed up by stocking suspenders, just in case . . . Remember, this implausible harness constituted only the underwear; it was of course necessary to add to it numerous external fineries. A young boy brought up in a strict family had not the faintest idea what the shape of a woman's body could possibly be, which plunged him into an abyss of confusion from which emerged all manner of fantastic hypotheses, each stranger and more convoluted than the one before. And things were not to improve with time because the woman of the 1900s was also subject to fashion which rearranged the natural form: strapped into a murderous corset which sawed at her groin, she seemed a victim of an anatomical architect's sadistic whimsy. One improvement had taken place: she had abandoned her "bustle," the molded false bottom which protruded like a shelf from the top of her derriere. To this day, no one can tell why they were considered de rigueur in the first place, and they were not to survive as an essential element of style for long. The building where I caroused as a child (and it was not in 1890, thank you very much!) belonged to an old woman, shriveled, and greedy, who wore proudly un-

continued on page 17

War of repression: from yesterday's corset to today's bondage, the evolution was logical...

Odette Joyeux "For One Night of Love" 1946.

"The Tall Man."

Martine Carol "Nana" 1954.

Fans of old-fashioned underwear worship the goddesses of the naughty frou-frou; pictured here are Martine Carol, Claudia Cardinale, and Suzy Delair.

Claudia Cardinale
"The Love Makers" 1961.

Suzy Delair "Jenny Lamour" 1947.

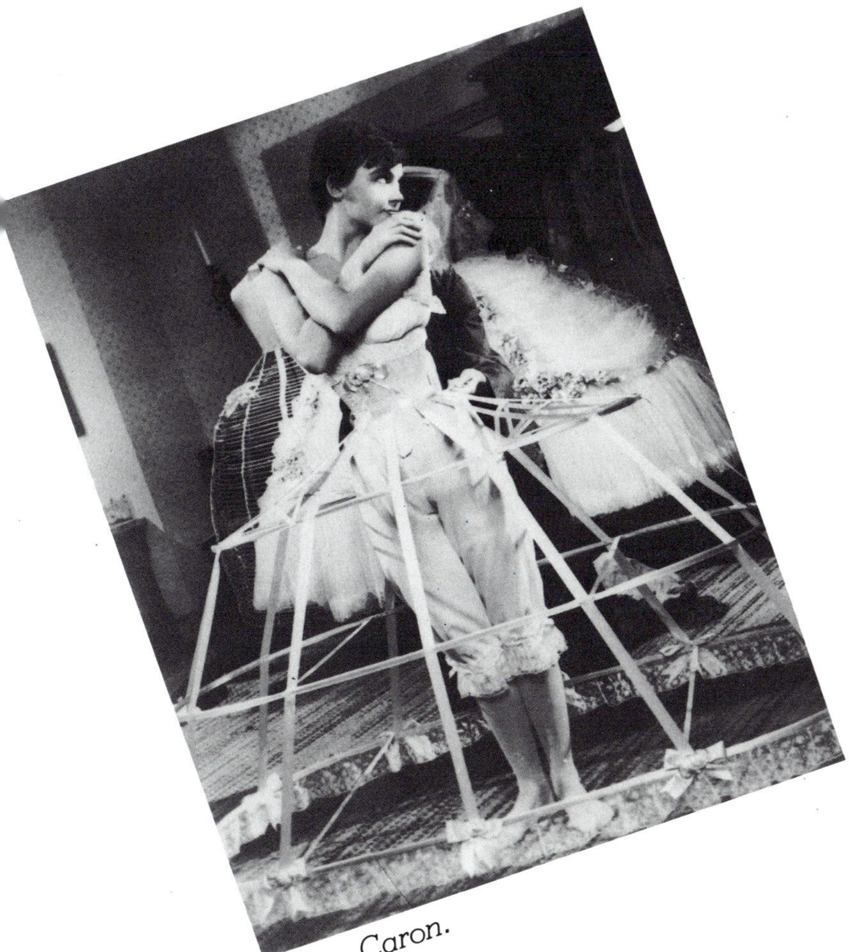

Leslie Caron.

der her shapeless dress a fake bottom and fake bosoms, covered over with pink satin. The fake bosoms, thinking they were real, had a vexing tendency to fall, which was really the last straw, so she adopted the habit of hoisting them back up with a swift gesture during our conversations. Even more surprising than that, the angrier she would become (and she was often angry, since children playing in a courtyard cause quite a ruckus), the more often her bosoms took the plunge, forcing her to frantically push them back into position, all the while roaring at the children's mischief. Her false derriere held up much better, however; it must have been welded on by force of habit, and we never had the pleasure of seeing it plummet to the pavement . . .

"Paris Will Always Be Paris" 1951.

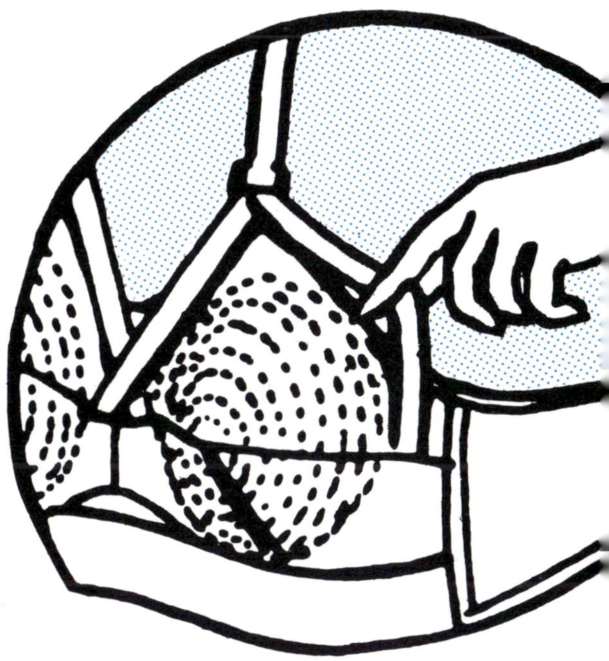

The only bright spots in this dark dance hall are the three charming bottoms wrapped in white, keeping the beat and the center of attention.

Changing styles will never alter the fact that there will always be stubborn people who believe that yesterday was better, and who adhere to the tenet that as long as something can be used, it should never be thrown away. There must be people who are still actively a part of that past, who still wear the strange antiquities of almost a century ago under their clothing. One would need the conscience and drive of a professional second-hand dealer to ferret out the novelty underthings, though, that might be found deep in the countrysides of the world.

In 1900 a woman was shaped like an S. In "The Nude Dressed and Undressed," Jacques Laurent, who seems to be somewhat of an authority in the field of feminine underwear, claims that the appearance of the hourglass figure contributed largely to filling up the consultation room of "Uncle Sigmund" (as he was popularly called), perhaps better known as Sigmund Freud, who was already on his way to becoming an institution. According to Laurent, the works of Freud concerning sexual repression cannot be dissociated from the period; "Underwear had, for the first time, the goal of opposing itself to loving impulses, materializing an interdiction which cannot help but have moved the clientele of Dr. Freud." During the development of psychoanalysis, style began to evolve: dresses became shorter, the corset gave way to the girdle or to the garter belt, the bra was elaborated, and the bloomer began to resemble our dear little panty. Curious young boys, however, have made little progress. A woman's silhouette has become naturalized, almost to the point of being without any understructure at all, and he no longer associates the weaker sex with a race of tortured aliens. However, since he is surrounded by pornographic magazines full of women posed in underwear, he is still hard pressed to make head or tail of anything. There are, in full view, two arms, two legs and a head similar to his own, but certain areas of their bodies, those particularly mysterious ones, are hidden by expertly crafted odds and ends, black, white or in color. And the agonizing question the kid immediately asks himself is: but under the underwear, for god's sake, what's under the underwear?

Despite his ignorance, he knows that the chest and the stomach of the alluring little coquettes are not made like his and, hidden in a closet, candle in hand, he destroys his retina trying to uncover the secret of underwear. It is then that one of his knowledgeable buddies proposes a trade: twelve Latin compositions for a magazine filled with girls naked from head to toe: word of honor. Deal. One month later, our young hero is full of hope as he locks himself in his closet and opens the forbidden work. Then, total stupefaction: they are naked, but nothing else! As far as the chest goes, two smooth impersonal globes, and then, below the stomach, a strange no-man's land, a sort of bald swelling, smooth as a knee, with slightly blurred outlines . . . It is the woman without bosoms and without sex, artfully modified by an unknown retoucher, whose curious profession consists of erasing from a woman's body all that could identify it. In the name of modesty and decency, the sanity of poor little boys was being challenged. Boys were appalled by this trickery, by this unhealthy illusion which tended to make them think that the feminine body was in all respects identical to that of his little sister's dolls. One must recognize that the "dirty" magazines and lingerie catalogs of the period failed to answer any of the questions being asked by the normal adolescent who was fascinated by anything having to do with sex.

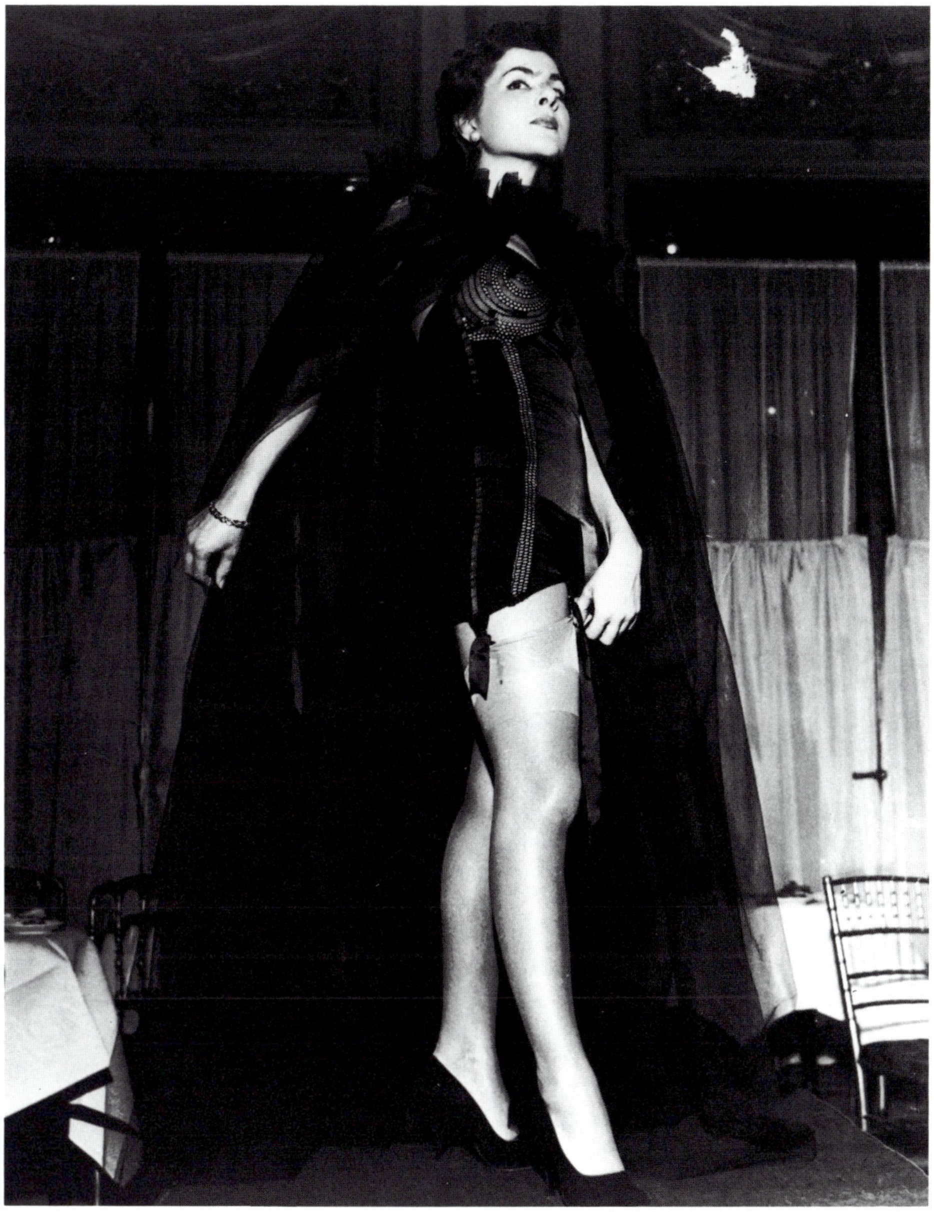

Lingerie. 1957.

Lingerie. 1957.

Wacky lingerie parades through the halls of a hotel full of strange little creatures...

X-rated newspapers and magazines have evolved to the point where even the most myopic and least aware young gentleman is able to immediately grasp the secrets of female anatomy, sprawled beneath his gaze in the finest detail. But the catalogs? Today there still exist thousands of uptight families whose offspring have only the lingerie pages of the huge publications issued by mail-order companies at their disposal for learning about the facts of life. Countless numbers of kids, just like that little boy of the early 1900s, continue to ask themselves what is underneath the underwear and what is it for? Why don't big girls wear the same underpants as they do, and are their strange and complicated underthings part of a mysterious rite whose initiation ceremonies are forbidden to curious little men? What on earth could a girdle be used for, and why wear a strapless bra with uplifting halfcups? Their heads full of question mark-shaped garter belts, hundreds of children carefully cut out the silhouettes that obsess them from outdated catalogs, pasting the figures into their notebooks for later ruminations during math class. They will grow out of this sweet obsession as soon as the day comes when they can satisfy their legitimate curiosity by closely examining the underwear of their little cousins or classmates. But some boys will never get over it. The world is swarming with panty fetishists, whose developments have been arrested at various levels, and who are incapable of keeping their wits about them in front of a fine lin-

continued on page 22

gerie shop window. And then there is the one who is content to look with the glazed eyes of Charles Denners in "The Man Who Loved Women" (and their underwear), but who is unable to dissociate the little vacant panty propped in front of him from that which is destined to fill it. What woman will buy this orphan fitted corselet, a redhead, a brunette, or a blond? And he would so like to be present when she tries it on, like a mouse hidden in the dressing room, not missing one crumb of the show. He would hear the delicious whisper of pearly fabric against the skin, the small sound of a zipper being done up fumblingly in the back, the thoughtful silence of the customer looking at herself in the mirror, still hesitating. Then he would whisper to her: "Oh yes madame! Buy it, and let's go christen it together at the Hotel of Happiness where, by my ardor, I will convince you of the wisdom of your choice!" Others collect the undergarments of those women they have dearly loved. It is enough for them to open the doors of a closet-safe, and instantly memories rush out like waves of heat. Martine's pink brassiere, Paula's leg garter, Monique's black slip and, faded by repeated washings, Mary's frilled beige panties. By accumulating traces of their past loves and keeping this tangible proof of them close at hand, they know that when they have become old, these glorious trophies will attest to their virility, and reassure them that they have spent their lives well. Then there are those who do not hesitate to steal the objects of their concupiscence from small shops and off of laundry lines, where they flap about in the wind; and since these have been worn, so much the better. In this fashion some accumulate formidable caches of delicate treasures, giving them sweet reasons to live . . .

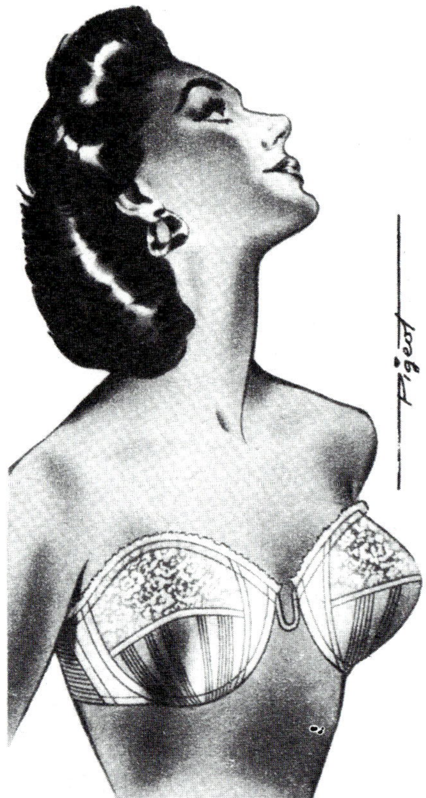

Réf. 5044
Un élégant soutien-gorge en dentelle Nylon doublée voile Nylon, avec bretelles amovibles, d'une adhérence totale, où le gansage du bonnet rehausse et maintient parfaitement la poitrine. Dos en tulle Lastex donnant le maximum d'aisance et de souplesse. Nouvelle armature flexplate garantie TARWIL, brevetée.

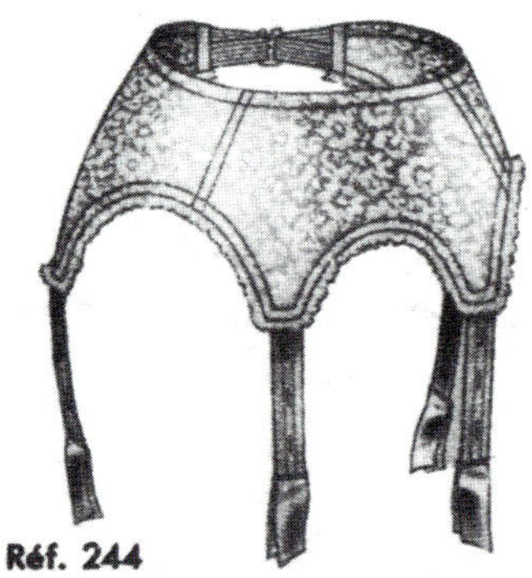

Réf. 244
Un porte-jarretelles en dentelle Nylon doublée voile Nylon, spécialement mis au point pour maintenir les bas bien à leur place.

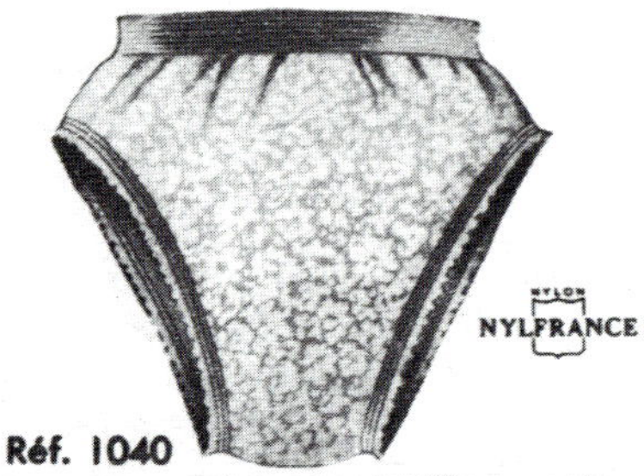

Réf. 1040
Le très seyant SLIP-LEJABY 'ÉQUILIBRÉ' en dentelle Nylon doublée jersey Nylon, parfaitement étudié dans toutes les tailles pour donner le maximum de confort.

Jean-Luc Hennig is a connoisseur of lingerie catalogs. He enjoys taking his time, leafing through each page, since he prefers the naked when it is dressed. Underwear, sensible or fanciful, gives him a big thrill. And although models in the lingerie section of modern catalogs are dressed in the sexiest of underthings, they often seem to have nothing worth hiding under the underwear. If they did have the knowing look of she who had something to hide, they would be far too provocative, too seductive to enter the average home. So they shine with health, sexy as a nudist camp, clean, innocent and sporty. It is certain they exercise every morning and eat yogurt, lots of yogurt. Their look is frank and direct. There are no panties in the back of their minds, no secret thoughts. And when there are no secret thoughts, of course, there is no eroticism. Except for those sports oriented types who revel in locker rooms filled with sweaty female jocks, but that's another story entirely. The innocent bottom is typically modern. During the beginning of the century, on the other hand, sexual taboos were still plentiful, and, as always, those taboos were incitements to debauchery . . .

Francoise Arnoul
"Forbidden Fruit" 1952.

Nothing was pure, according to our grandpas, who were the great champions in all categories of puritanism. They saw evil everywhere and, consequently, evil flourished, delighted that so much attention was being paid to it. Everything served as a pretext for censorship and tight surveillance. Bloomers that descended to the knees, made of a light fabric and worn underneath skirts and petticoats, set off violent polemics beginning in the middle of the 19th century. Two questions followed one another in immutable order: should women wear bloomers and, if so, should they be open or closed? "Open, open, from the front to the back" clamored the gentlemen who recognized in the closed bloomer yet another obstacle to the expression of their sentiments. No one was upset by the corsets, the garter belts, the under-bodices, the camisoles, the slips, the leg garters. Even though women were wearing heaps of batiste and waves of lace under their everyday outfits, it remained easy for those who were romantically persistent to roll the whole costume up with one deft maneuver, taking advantage of direct access to a woman's secret charms before the lass even understood what was happening to her! As the feminine panty became popular, the sexually obsessed realized that this posed them with a stickier problem than they were used to: they were going to need twenty times more slyness and audacity to seduce the reticent lady whom they desired. Imagine a sweetheart laying in your arms; perhaps she shouldn't be there at all (if her husband ever found out!), but at the same time it feels so good, and all things considered, the act itself has not yet been consummated. She is thus not yet a fallen woman. With a hunter's instinct, you feel that her resistance is weakening, as she repeatedly sighs "No, no, it's no good, we musn't." But the words are empty of meaning. In fact, she is no longer thinking, and is interested only in prolonging the pleasure of the kiss. This is the seducer's most hopeful script. But if she is wearing underwear which has no opening or affords no easy access, nothing works anymore! The most important instant, the magic moment when it is necessary to act, is dangerously compromised. In the time it takes to find the closing mechanism of the bloomer, to untie it, to slip the thin cloth down her thigh, the sinner has regained her senses and realizes that she was in danger of allowing herself to be taken advantage of. The spell is broken. All you can do is put your clothes back on . . .

In his "picturesque history of the feminine panty," author Romi declares that the panty's original debut must be attributed to the illustrious dancers of the French cancan. These charming girls lifted their legs so high that a special covering around the bottom's cheeks was an absolute necessity in order to avoid showing them at each move. The panty quickly became mandatory for performing this dance, which in and of itself is an apology for under-

continued on page 26

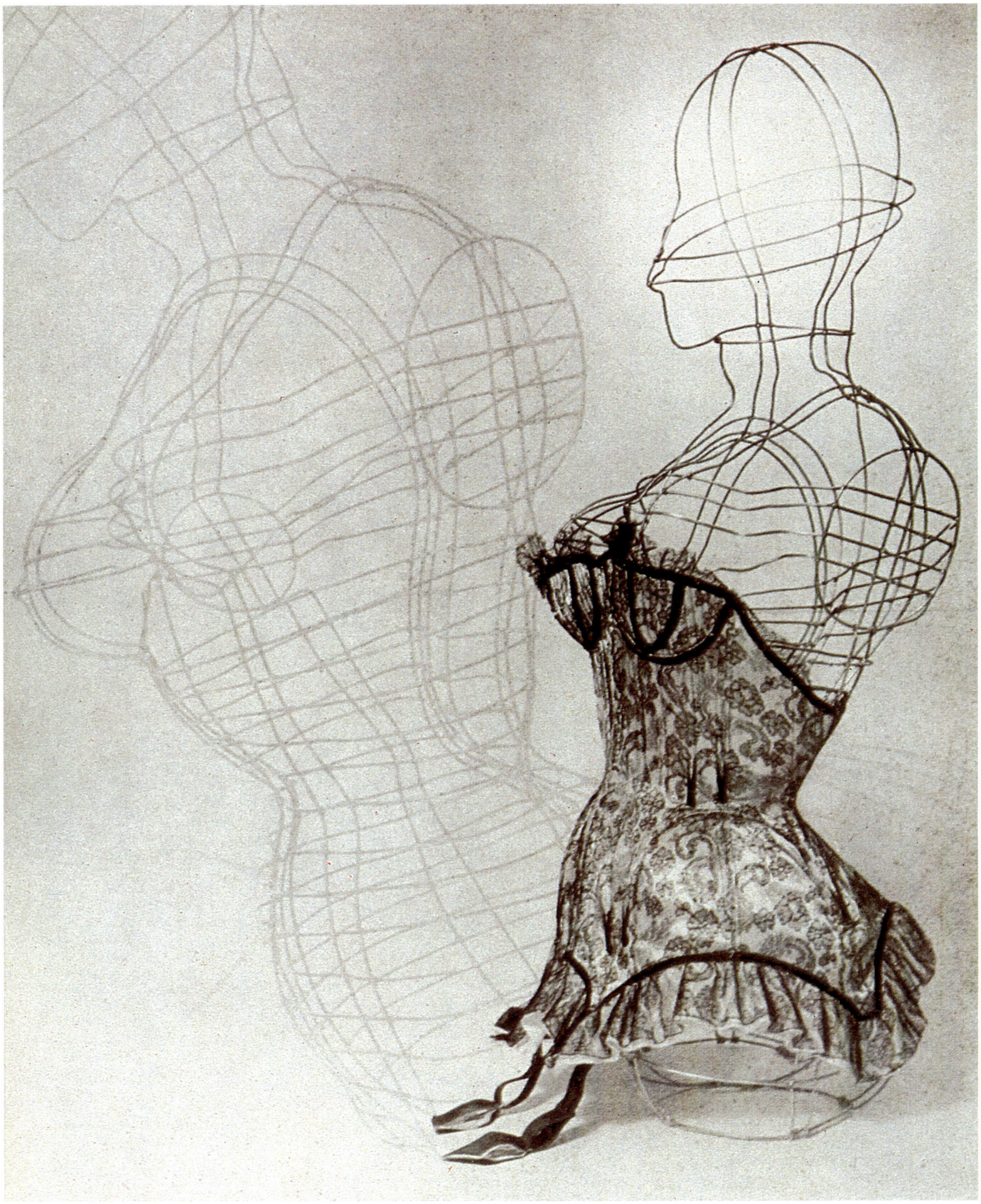

Bustier. 1945.

wear. The coquettes, doubtless inspired by their own wicked dance, were quick to select open models, very open, so as to titillate the gentlemen in the first rows, who maintained their vigilant watch for the sudden disclosure of what lay beyond the lace. All this was not to the taste of the censors, who had imposed the panty in the name of decency, and not in order to arouse cancan dancers and watchers alike. Action was taken. The chief of police appointed a "panty inspector" whose sole responsibility was to prevent dancers from "displaying their natural charms." Every night, his pockets full of safety pins, "father modesty" inspected the dancers who were ready to go on stage. Woe to those panties which featured excessively long slits! They were mercilessly pinned back together by the incorruptible official. If a series were created called "Picturesque Professions to Reinstate," one would have to award an honorable mention to the panty inspector, flanked by his colleague in censorship, the retoucher/eraser of feminine sexuality on paper. The two of them make a beautiful pair of killjoys. But as far as the enjoyment of one's job goes, they were, on the other hand, in an excellent position, and must have charming professional anecdotes to relate.

The panty was the uncontested star of the underwear world; everyone had something to say on the subject. And if what men said was almost always "no," it was not without reason. The open panty did not change anything, of course. Slit from the navel to the dimpling of the derriere, the panty was hardly a legitimate obstacle and did little to prevent certain occurences. It was the principle of the panty which scared men with any talent for predicting the future: from the open to the closed model required only a simple bit of sewing, a tiny little modification which was most certainly to follow. And the great seducers had every reason to be afraid: the panty was indeed closed up, shortly thereafter, for good. It was the end of the quickie. In the name of modesty and decency, that which had for centuries been open was now closed. This closing up of underwear was not without its difficulties. As soon as women tired of bloomers, towards 1928, they were to adopt the abbreviated bloomer, which

was invented for children.

But Morality did not only attack daytime underwear. It also interfered in the affairs of nighttime lingerie. Included in the trousseaus that well-raised young ladies were required to sew, there were, in addition to closed undies, pleated smocks made of buckram, or nightshirts made in a material that was only a slight improvement on sackcloth. These nightshirts ran all the way up the neck, down the arms to the wrists, and down the legs to the ankles. Armed with their scissors, these innocent young ladies opened a pocket at the level of the stomach which buttoned up at the waist like a kind of flap. It was obviously considered in poor taste to ask questions concerning the utility of this strange casement window, through which, on trying wedding nights, slightly tipsy husbands would take charge of the marital ritual, without even having taken the trouble to make an explanation such as "this gap, my dearest, was devised by prescient people to allow me to make you pregnant without ever having to touch your body, just in case you might enjoy it; better safe than sorry." Only the feet to trot to bed, the head to pray, and the hands to pick off a rosary, could emerge from the newlyweds' shrouds. To have a little fun, it was preferable to become a courtesan. Then one would have the most beautiful and the most expensive underwear in the world, in silk muslin, net, satin, light batiste, buckram, crepe or in organdy, with twinings of ribbons, favors, lace, ruffles, or embroidered flounces, everything the imagination of lingerie-makers and their customers could dream up, and that was extensive, to say the least. With courtesans, men made efforts at conversation and were much more attentive, generous and sustaining lovers.

While their husbands ruined themselves in brothels, bourgeois women resigned themselves to buying pretty camisole-like nightgowns for their children. These were, however, equipped with a device that restrained their hands so they could not touch themselves at night. *That* was sexy lingerie. What else could you do besides think about sex, think about it again, always think of it, without any foreseeable opportunity to actually do it?

"I GOT A LITTLE
BEHIND IN MY RENT"
NO
PARKING
PRINTED IN U. S. A.

A RUN ON SUGAR
A MUTOSCOPE CARD
PRINTED IN U. S. A.

"EVEN SANTA CAN'T FILL A STOCKING
BETTER THAN THAT"
PRINTED IN U. S. A

"HOW'D YOU LIKE TO
HOLD MY HAND?"
A MUTOSCOPE CARD
PRINTED IN U. S. A.

PHOTOPLAY PINUPS
MARILYN
MONROE
No. 4
35¢

Illustration by Vargas.

One personality from the "Golden Age" of Hollywood epitomizes this extreme puritanism—Will H. Hays, the creator of the Hays Censorship Code. He too was nicknamed the "father of modesty," but his job allowed him to bully an entire industry, not just a few can-can dancers. Hays reigned over the film world with the hard fist of a tyrant and the obsession of a religious cultist. From 1922 to 1945 directors were obliged to make films which under no circumstances violated the Hays Code. And it was not easy: the depiction of nudity, violence, passion, sex and exhibitionism was strictly forbidden, and Hays was vehemently opposed to the display of any part of the body's anatomy as well, especially the navel (it was later learned that he was not able to tell the difference between the sex and the navel of a woman, which drove his wife to ask for a divorce after years of suffering through his confusion). Scenes which incorporated undressing of almost any sort were forbidden, unless they were absolutely indispensable to the plot's development. The stars' underwear, needless to say, had to be copious, extremely concealing, and as long and opaque as possible.

continued on page 34

Viviane Romance "They Were Five" 1936.

Michele Morgan "The Proud and the Beautiful" 1953.

Arletty.

Suzy Delair
"Lady Paname" 1949.

In spite of her very extensive western underwear, the type that Hays preferred, Jane Russell looks perfectly equipped to corral any kind of Macho Man! "The Paleface" 1948.

Angie Dickinson
"Point Blank" 1967.

The use of underclothing in westerns was employed with vigor. Vast arrays of bloomers in white cotton were utilized (I leave you to guess if they were open or closed) to hide the stomach, bottom, thighs and knees of the actresses. And the navel, of course, I almost forgot the navel; excuse *me* Mr. Hays. Camisoles and the under-bodice were responsible for camouflaging the upper regions, so all that was left of the women was a little neck, quite a bit of arm and very little leg. This was also the period of the very dressed dishabille and the very studied negligee. The censors were so strict in their efforts to assure that underwear and lingerie would not traumatize the moralists that one could almost imagine a woman doing her grocery shopping in her underthings, so bulky and substantial had her garb become. In a word, underwear had to look like over-wear.

Any director who infringed upon these castrating laws was

continued on page 36

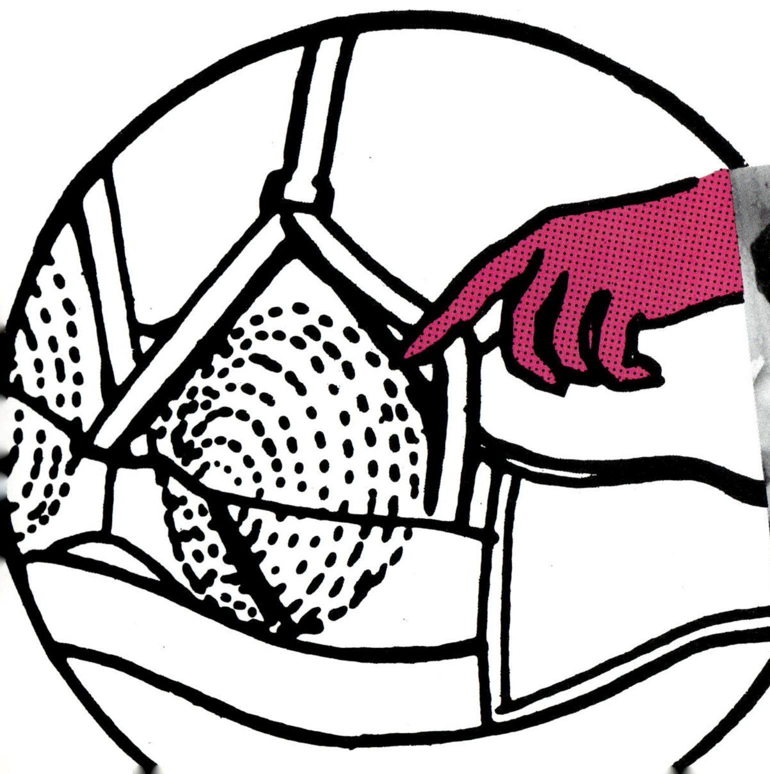

"This is Parisian Life" 1953.

blacklisted, and his films were never released. To top it all off, there was the terrifying "Legion of Catholic Decency," which existed independently of the Hays Code and which considered the Code to be too indulgent and called for a boycott of all films it had rated C (for "Condemned"). And it really was a condemnation: so strong was the catho-cinephobes' influence upon American families that any film the legion found displeasing was not distributed. Nicknamed the "Ku Klux Klan of the cinema," the Legion of Decency managed to drive to despair those directors who had been spared by Hays. Nothing less than World War II could have weakened the influence of these terrifying censorship boards.

One of the first big production films to defy the code was "The Outlaw," starring the fabulously endowed Jane Russell. When producer/director Howard Hughes met Jane in a train station (so the story goes) he immediately visualized the impact her 39" bust would have on the artistic sensibilities of masculine cinephiles. But it was still out of the question to openly defy the Code or for that matter the Legion, still ready to faint with horror at the slightest titillation. It was impossible to show too much of Jane's opulent chest without risking a ban on the showing of the movie. On the other hand, Hughes was determined to promote the move by capitalizing on the measurements of his star. Then he had a stroke of genius. Assembling all the knowledge of aeronautics he possessed, he sat down at his drawing table and created a revolutionary new bra which, with its specially studied aerodynamics, could propel Jane's endowments through any piece of clothing. The only remaining obstacle was filming the very suggestive but never daring scenes. The bra and Jane were both a hit, though the movie went unreleased for three years due to the board of censors, who had understood perfectly that they were being mocked. But there was no concrete evidence to keep the film from being seen. Jane's forbidden zones were never actually visible. With demonic skill, Hughes had arranged things so that Jane would appear to be dressed only in underclothing even though she never removed so much as a stitch. Her bra and blouse were so tight-fitting, so revealing, that one could not help thinking about what was underneath.

Audrey Hepburn "Monte Carlo Baby" 1951.

Simone Signoret "Casque d'or" 1951.

"Mademoiselle X".

"In The Kingdom of Heaven" 1950.

Movie stars at your service

Controversy. Such was the typical dilemma inspired by the undergarment. After the initial furor caused by movies of questionable intention, the censors were finally rendered ineffective due to the rapidly growing public objections. With the release of "The Outlaw" they were forced to admit their defeat. Tremendous success and terrific scandal were the results. From then on, the code was relaxed, and nudity, violence and sex began to infiltrate movie studios, timidly at first, then more openly. Producers were quick to realize that sexier films were more profitable than "clean" ones, and began to defend their right to make and see films without hypocrisy, telling real-life stories in all their brutality and passion. Obviously, underclothing was part of that reality. For years, directors had been obliged to hide all suggestion of nudity behind folding-screen-type arrangements. Now that they had the chance to present bare breasts and naked bottoms, filmmakers were certainly not going to pass by this new opportunity. Undergarments were to hold a new and more interesting place in the history of American film. Now that nudity was allowed, the director who chose to film a girl wearing a bra was indulging in a deliberate act which corresponded to a personal and significant statement. By losing its mandatory nature the undergarment recovered its

Ava Garaner.

personality and officially resumed its mischievous role; to awaken men's curiosity.

When an analytically minded movie-goer sees a girl wearing only panties, he no longer tells himself: "Okay, the director wanted her to be naked, but since he was not allowed, he put panties on her." He knows that underwear has historical importance, that the heroine should not be clothed otherwise, and that this underclothing gives her, depending upon the movie, a look of surprise, vulnerability, provocation, or anticipation. If the film is Italian, and the spectator is as well, he no longer questions, he simply enjoys. Italy has always reveled in suggestive underwear, both in its film stars and as the private objects of desire. The romantic Italian is easily seduced by the garter belt, and quite enamored of panties. There are hundreds of Italian movies featuring a wide range of pretty girls in underwear. There is even an actress, Gloria Guida, whose entire career was based upon her remarkable ability to wear her panties in both an innocent and perverse fashion simultaneously. It made Italian machos go wild. The unselfish director shares the pleasure he has taken in shooting the undressing scenes with the spectator. No great Italian actress ever avoided the test to see how spectacularly she could display an undergarment. In the "Sacred Monsters" series, Sophia Loren took the cake with her famous striptease in "Yesterday, Today and Tomorrow." The combination of her talent with her

continued on page 40

Silvana Pampanini.

Susan Cabot
"Ride Clear of Diablo" 1954.

Joan Collins
"Rally Round the Flag Boys"
1959.

outfit, including a fitted corselet, with garters, uplifting brassiere, panties and stockings, all in black lace, created one of the most beautiful and electrifying striptease scenes ever to appear on the screen. Sophia made a variety of other films in which she appears in fanciful under-finery, particularly in "The Millionairess," in which she wears a fabulous black leather fitted corselet. Oh, the whims of rich women! Claudia Cardinale also excited enthusiasts of the corset and other old-fashioned undergarments when she played the part of a prostitute in "The Love Makers." During this film, Cardinale strutted around in a turn-of-the-century camisole, black corset clasped in front, white slip with a large flounce, flesh-colored stockings, crumply garter and little lace-trimmed black socks. If you like that style, you'll surely get your money's worth.

The third hands down winner in the lingerie hall of fame is, of course, Gina Lollobrigida, *the* Lollobrigida, who, so as not to disappoint her army of admirers, would occasionally display her lovely breasts. In "Fanfan the Tulip" she does a charming number in outdated but hardly passé underwear. The provocative way she wears this lingerie has a lot to do with her perennial charm.

Sophia Loren
"Yesterday Today and Tomorrow"
1964.

Shirley MacLaine
"Woman Times Seven"
1967.

Jayne Mansfield "Kiss them for me" 1957.

Jayne Mansfield and her built-for-fantasy bustline, calling all fans. Oh mama! Just leave your name and number...

FOLIES DE
Paris et Hollywood
BELLES D'AUTOMNE
85 NUS
30 COULEURS NATURELLES

In the pastel palaces made of cardboard paste and whipped cream that Hollywood built to make people dream, one's search for those abominable family portraits hung on the walls would be in vain. In the world of entertainment, there are no dull princesses with peevish faces; rather, the artists' portraits comprise a fabulous array of succulent, smiling beauties, offering fleshy, curvy figures to the eyes of the spectator, unveiling the soft lines of their lightly clothed bodies. All the stars and starlets of Hollywood's harem are there, posing for posterity with the legitimate desire to show their very best to their adoring fans, past, present and future. The court photographers, sensitive to the softness of their sweet charms, fixed them for eternity on prettily colored backgrounds, respecting the velvety smoothness of the wonderfully attired models...

Marilyn Monroe.

Hanna Schygulla "The Marriage of Maria Braun" 1978.

Gina Lollobrigida "Fast and Sexy" 1958.

Claudia Cardinale
"Love and Kisses from Athens"

Gina, Sophia and Claudia instilled sexy underwear with a true sense of nobility, by wearing it not as if it was an encumbering and frustrating necessity but rather as charm revealers. And the new Italian stars share this wonderful talent with their predecessors. Ornella Mutti, Laura Antonelli, and Agostina Belli already display the proper dispositions when it comes to underwear. Remember "Malicia," in which Laura made the spectator nervous as soon as he laid eyes on a poster . . . In France, looking underneath things can easily become intellectualized. In Alain Robbe-Grillet's "The Immortal Woman," Françoise Brion wears a fitted corselet and stockings of a somber eroticism, as dark as death. In "I Love You, Me Neither," Jane Birkin's little white panties are enough all by themselves to explain why Jane would make a perfect little boy, and it is this ambiguity that seduces a homosexual, who is attracted by the total absence of femininity that she displays, in her appearance as well as in her choice of underwear. Stranger and even more unhealthy is the film "Love Doll," by Luis Garcia Berlanga, a Spanish director brought up by Jesuits. I don't know whether it is due to his Jesuit training or a product of that famous Spanish puritanism, but the film reaches real depths of tragedy and sordidness quite beyond all farce. Michel Piccoli plays the part of a dentist who increasingly ignores his wife, while turning his attention to a synthetic life-size doll, which he dresses up in naughty underwear and loves more than his real woman. Hello fetishism, not to mention misogyny. The movie was too disturbing to ever become a commercial success, but in addition to presenting a surprising and curious aspect of the use of underwear, it is an interesting documentation of perversion.

Sophia Loren. 1967.

Gina Lollobrigida
"The Dolls" 1965.

Laura Antonelli "Malicia" 1973.

Sophia Loren "The Millionairess" 1960.

"Splendor in the Grass" 1961.

Jeanne Moreau "The Wolverines" 1957.

Jeanne Valerie in the early Sixties.

Raquel Welch. "Myra Breckinridge" 1969.

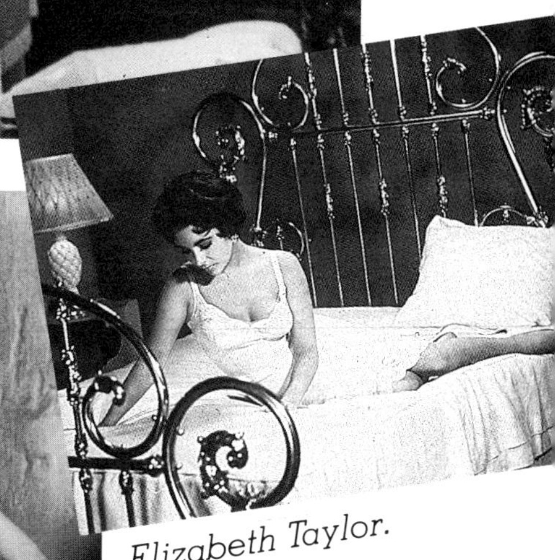

Elizabeth Taylor.

Raquel Welch
"The Oldest Profession" 1967.

Raquel Welch
"100 Rifles" 1968.

Pornographic movies, at least those that maintain vague aesthetic pretensions and some sort of logical structure, do not shy away from hiding for a moment something they intend to show later on in all its detail. Fitted corselets, garter belts, waist cinchers, corsets and cleverly low-cut body-suits are all frequent accessories in X-rated movies with any kind of budget. Funds, however, are usually as minimal as the storyline (or the underclothing, for that matter). Better to turn to legitimate erotic cinema, which utilizes a great deal of extremely imaginative under-attire. Films like "Emmanuelle," "The Story of O," and "The Eleven Thousand Rods," gave enchanted spectators refreshing visions of superb girls frolicking about in superb decors. With beautiful photography and careful lighting, these films never went beyond the stage of the softest porn. Emmanuelle, who looks like the type who would go pantyless under her garter belt, enjoyed enormous success. Throughout the world, crowds would rush headlong to see her slip off her stockings, whispering to her panting husband: "This morning I made love twelve times to a delicious couple in the club's dressing room." The "Story of O" was a somewhat awkward and stilted film, but garnished with a display of wondrous underwear, making it pleasant enough to see anyway. As for "The Eleven Thousand Rods," violence and pornography that had been included in the Apollinaire text was toned down by a commercial desire on the part of the director, Eric Lipmann. To compensate for this censorship, he invested a great deal in underwear, so that his movie sometimes resembled an extended commercial for fine lingerie commissioned by a garment manufacturers' union. But all the precautions and surface propriety could not stop the censorship commission, and, in 1974, a prohibition upon all hard and soft porn films was put into effect, with no distinctions made between pleasant sensual fantasies and hard core films. The French release of "Emmanuelle II" was blocked for a long time by censors who had firmly decided to rate the film "X." Movie producers were quick to understand the lesson, and since soft porn cost much more to produce than hard-core, they simply discontinued the genre without a second thought. Nowadays, if you want to find panties and lingerie used in an intelligent way, you should go to horror movies or sci-fi flicks, in which dreadful monsters and wicked sadists love to plunder the silky underwear of their innocent victims before they are eaten! Because horror movies are usually filled with thinly disguised sexual connotations, the undergarment, with all its symbolic weight, could not escape the fantasies of directors. If the moment of attack was meant to affect viewers as effectively as possible—and after all, that's what they were there for—it was strategically sound to suffuse the scene that preceded the act of violence with sweetness and nonchalance. Not only does this ploy provide unnerving suspense, but it also gives dramatic resonance to the horror of the aggression. Vampires for example, who only operate after sunset, often surprise their negligee clad prey while she's sleeping peacefully or pounce while the victim is busy getting ready for bed, wearing next to nothing, of course! In my opinion, one of the most beautiful and striking scenes to appear in a horror film takes place in Ridley Scott's terrifying "Alien." An indestructible monster makes its way into a spaceship and massacres every crew member one by one. The only survivor, the beautiful "Ripley," finally escapes in an emergency spacecraft. After an hour and a half of tension and horror, the heroine, as well as the entire movie-house, breathe a "whew" of relief. This girl deserved to have her life spared, and when she undresses to get some rest, it is with tenderness that we look at her regulation underclothes: matching undershirt and briefs. There is nothing sexy about military underwear. Except, perhaps, when it is worn by Ripley, but she is so frightened, and so is the audience, that . . . Gasp! The tension just shot up like an arrow: the Alien is hiding in the emergency ship, and Ripley is unwittingly bringing it back to earth, as a souvenir . . . and she is in her underpants, the poor girl, underpants and undershirt made of 100% cotton, while facing her is this monster excreting his acids and bad intentions from every orifice! Personally, I've had a lot of trouble

X

Liza Minnelli "Cabaret" 1972.

Mylene Demongeot "Under Ten Flags" 1960.

forgetting these images, and it seemed very dangerous to me to walk around my bedroom in my panties and T-shirt. The monster could be anywhere, in a closet, under the bed, and there isn't even a life-vest within reach.

For a change of pace, I went to see "An Unmarried Woman," in which Jill Clayburgh deals with New York's summer heat by dressing in panties and T-shirt and lounging about her large and cheerful bay-windowed apartment. The simple albeit chic combination of T-shirt and panties has often inspired those directors who are enthusiasts of the realism of young modern women. The full-slip, on the other hand, is less tempting. In the first place, it is not abbreviated and therefore less attractive than other varieties of underwear. Also, the type of movies in which actresses walk around in slips tend to be on the morose side. Look at Romy Schneider. You can't say that directors cast her in many funny films. For the most part, they were dramas, films of suffering and catastrophe, and, unfortunately, similar to her own life experiences. When you saw her undressed in a movie, it was always in a slip. In "The Infernal Trio," "The Important Thing is to Love," "The Old Rifle" (where she ends up being fried alive no less, with flame throwers!), as well as in "The Train," we find Romy in a slip and in a desperate situation.

On stage the actress wears a provocative outfit and is in command. In her everyday panties, however, she feels naked and fragile.

Even though it is about as sexy as a school blouse, can the slip really bring bad luck?

There are, however, some very pretty slip styles as well: smooth and silky, perfectly cut, and so well made that they could glide through a ballroom without seeming at all out of place. The ordinary slip, on the other hand, is the sensible dress-lining type, creased and wrinkled around the stomach, and generally lacking in style. Even in school I refused to wear one. It would become twisted no matter which way it was adjusted and, like any typical synthetic, it would go all the way up my thighs and bunch up around my waist when I walked quickly. Not a great feeling. School was hell when it came to underclothes. At first, we were all wearing old-fashioned briefs that wouldn't shrink even when boiled, so there was equality and fraternity in the playground. Then, in chronological order, came little pink panties, purely decorative brassieres, and garter belts. Fools like me attempted to hide their plump little bodies behind these disfiguring prehistoric briefs, which were too white, too thick, and worst of all, ended up too high at the waist. The day the most popular girl in the class showed up wearing stockings there was a revolution in the locker room. Stunned with admiration for her beautiful brown stockings that made her look one hundred years older, we were all drooling with jealousy, and damning the socks that kept us in the kiddie category, even though we wore panties and trainer bras. Dozens of us suddenly discovered a strange ailment known as cold knees, and it became urgent for us to buy stockings, for fear of freezing to death! Garters, and stockings that ran as soon as we slipped them on were finally ours. Post-swimming pool dressing sessions in tiny, overcrowded cubicles became epic battles between recalcitrant nylons and our chlorine-water-bloated legs; but we were so thrilled to look at last like real women that everything else seemed unimportant . . .

Sigourney Weaver "Alien" 1979.

P. Medina "Phantom of the rue Morgue" 1954

Marlene Jobert "The Passenger of the Rain" 1969.

"The Man Who Loved Women" 1977.

Claudia Cardinale
"The Love Makers" 1961.

Romy Schneider
"The Train" 1973.

Jane Fonda "Joy House" 1964.

Beneath her still-childlike curves, Jane Fonda makes her debut in babydolls, already exhibiting the talents of a strong-willed actress.

Corrine Clery "The Story of O" 1976.

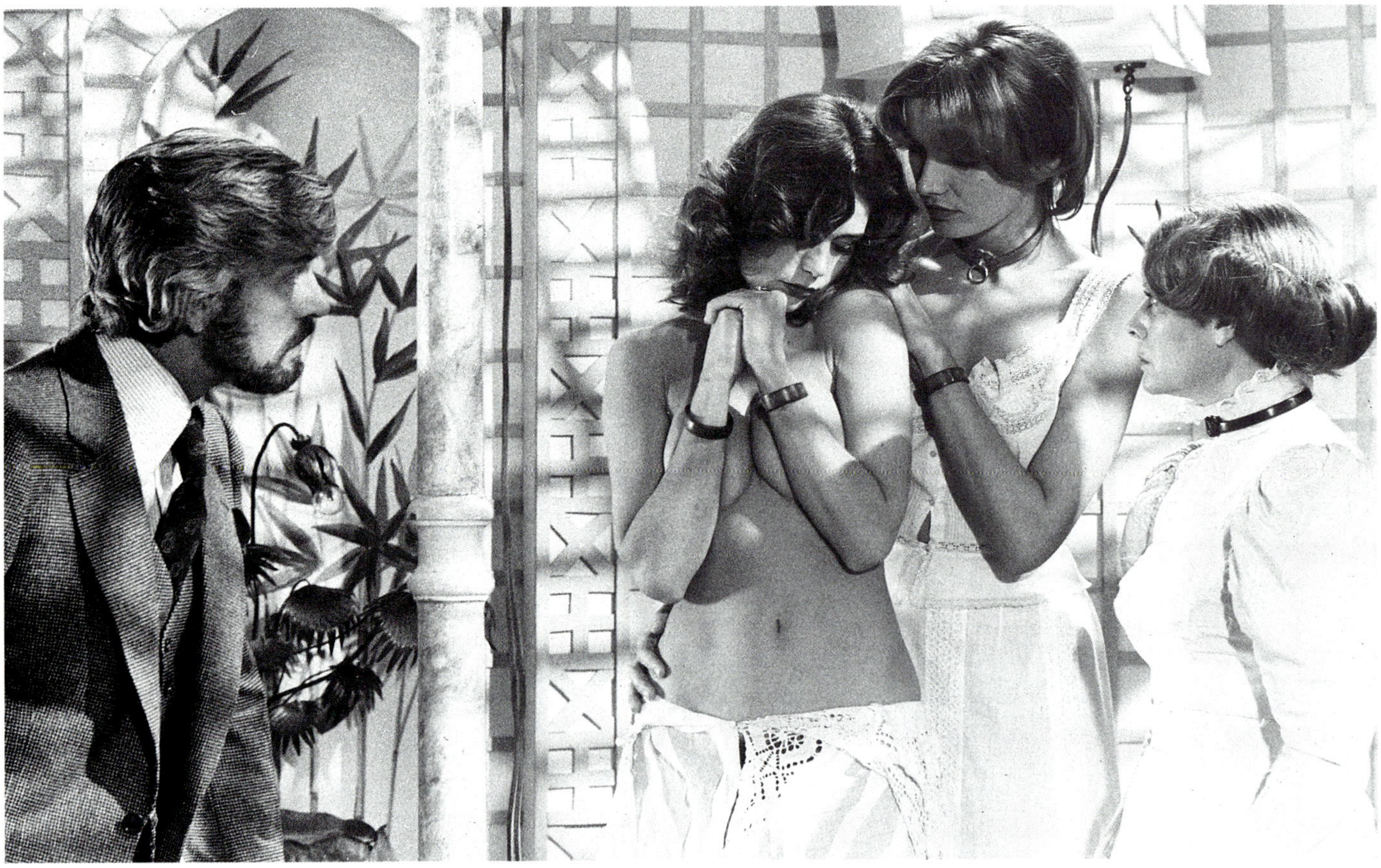

Catherine Deneuve "Mississippi Mermaid" 1968.

Carole Bouquet "That Obscure Object of Desire" 1977.

Sylvia Kristel "The Adultress" 1968.

"Sex at the Office"

From soft-core to hard-core, sex movies gladly use underwear of all types and tastes, especially naughty...

Brooke Shields and
Susan Sarandon
"Pretty Baby" 1978.

Brooke Shields in "Pretty Baby," which the French called "La Petite" 1978.

In France the film was called "American College." American audiences remember it as "Animal House" 1978.

"The Schoolgirl and the Doctor"

Michel Piccoli "Love Doll" 1974.

"Baba Vaga".

"Madame Claude 2" 1980.

Barbara Bouchet "Fainting Spells"

Marilyn in fishnets

Stupefaction. That's what our reaction would have been if we had been told, back then, that Jean Harlow and Marilyn Monroe boasted about how they wore nothing underneath their clothes. What do you mean, nothing? Not even a pair of panties? In other words, they were walking around naked in the street! Heavens! All you had to do was open your eyes to notice that some of Marilyn's dresses seemed glued to her skin, that even the most miniscule panties hadn't the slightest chance of being discreetly slipped on underneath . . . However, the famous scene that made her lower anatomy legendary required that she wear some underwear; otherwise there would not have been crowds but riots. Standing over a subway vent, she whispers, in her soft voice, about how good it feels to get a little air, and every time the subway goes by, her dress scurries up over those long legs.

With each torrid gust, we catch a glimpse of a little (or sometimes a lot) of the very modest panties she wears that match the color of her dress. All the hardiest men in New York were there the night of the shooting, gathered behind the barricades, praying for another take to be called for. Only one man was made uncomfortable by this scene, and all the hustle and bustle around it: his name was Joe DiMaggio, and he was married to Marilyn at the time. He could not put up for long with a wife who, ninety percent of the time, didn't wear underwear, and, when it was called for in a specific role, would display it to everyone. But that was not the end of "The Seven Year Itch." In another interesting scene, Marilyn explains to her downstairs neighbor—actor Tom Ewell—that when the weather is really hot, she keeps her underclothes cool, and if he would be kind enough to wait five minutes, she will go take her panties out of the freezer. The unsuspecting chap promptly tuns green and chokes. He has doubtless imagined Marilyn's burning bottom, slipping into frozen panties, and the thermal shock scrambles his brains . . . That's pure hot and cold Monroe. How could any man resist? Would you like some more panty in your whisky?

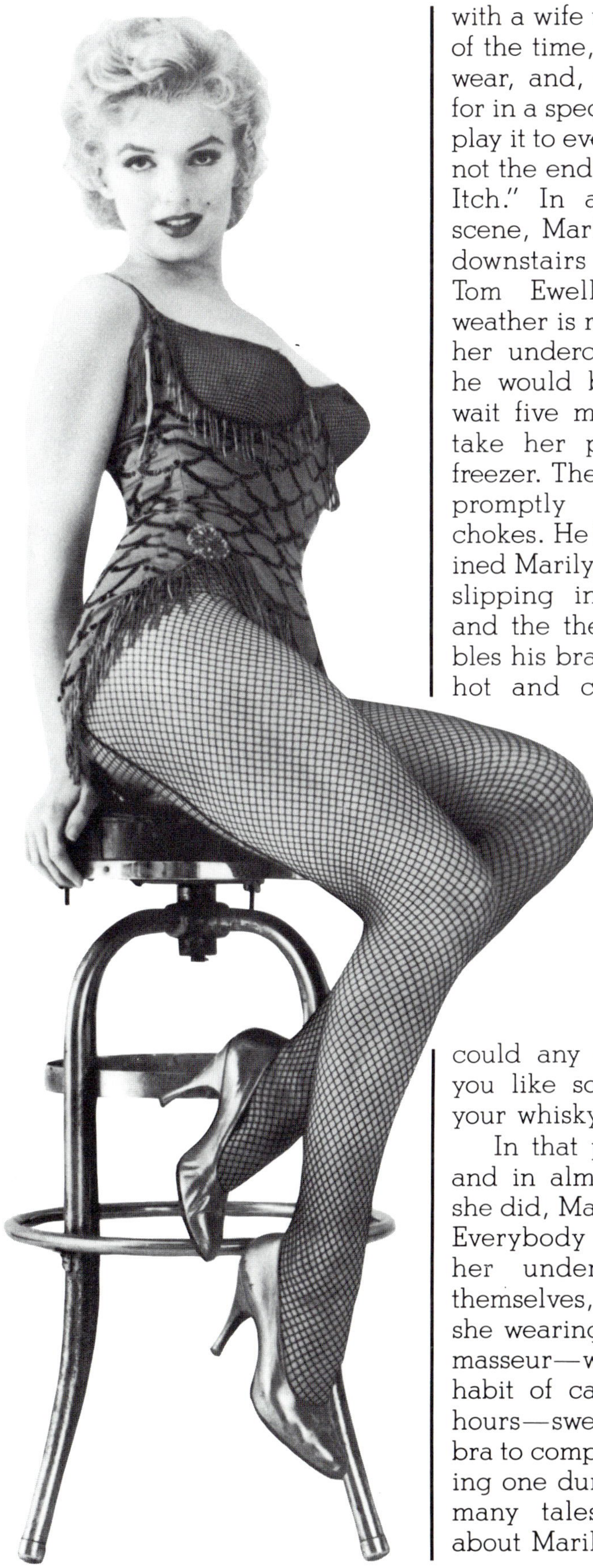

In that particular instance, and in almost everything else she did, Marilyn was a success. Everybody was interested in her underwear and asked themselves, "Now, is she or isn't she wearing any?" Her private masseur—whom she was in the habit of calling at impossible hours—swears she slept in a bra to compensate for not wearing one during the day. But so many tales have been told about Marilyn . . .

Marilyn Monroe.

Bardot unveils her charms

Loving her roles just as much as Marilyn had, Brigitte Bardot is another infamous sex-symbol who enjoyed trotting around in the buff, but sported underwear just as divinely. In "And God Created Woman," for example, she imprisoned her perfect body in a white fitted corselet which had the wonderful result of showing off beautiful, tempting breasts. The wasp-waisted strapless corset is a pleasant invention when it comes to special effects. The bones of the brassiere, particularly surrounding the bosom, suited Brigitte well, and she would wear them often. In "The Light Across the Street" however, her charms are hampered by a sinister slip, and guess what? The movie turns out badly. So you see, I told you dull slips foretell unhappy endings! One might write a thesis on the pernicious influence of long ugly slips on films in which they prevail. All this brings to mind "Cat on a Hot Tin Roof," a film which did not exactly belong to the happy musical category either. With its heavy atmosphere, high tension, and repressed sense of violence, one might say that Liz Taylor was perfectly attired in her chaste white slip. Seriously now, there are underthings which are far more frightful:

continued on page 67

Brigitte Bardot.

Brigitte Bardot.

As the object of men's desire, underwear can generate conflict and get women into trouble...

Brigitte Bardot
"And God Created Woman"
1956.

Brigitte Bardot
"The Novices" 1970.

the garter belt, for example. One cannot discuss the underwear glamour girls of the cinema without mentioning Marlene Dietrich and her famous killer-garter in "The Blue Angel." The sensual vulgarity of Lola leads a venerable professor to the other side of madness, tortured as he is already by a late mid-life crisis. Lola's singing number, performed by Marlene in ruffled panties, risqué garter belt and black stockings, is a nice piece of history that all underwear fans know by heart—from the smutty snap of the elastic just before the show, to Dietrich's inimitable style of singing, with just the right dose of scorn and provocation. But one must not neglect the panty scene, which is of pivotal importance to the development of the plot. In Lola's dressing room, a child snatches the singer's panties and stuffs them in his strict professor's pocket. The next day, in the midst of a lesson, the professor reaches for his handkerchief, hidden in the depths of his coat; what he pulls from his pocket instead is the wrinkled pair of panties, which, needless to say, causes a tremendous uproar. This incident with the panties is the old professor's first step toward complete moral decay, and it's all so sinister that you must have a taste for life to bear with the movie until the end. And all of this because of some stolen pair of panties and an ill-famed garter belt. This movie shows the darker side of underwear, and one must see a lot of cheerfully naughty movies to forget that undergarments can sometimes lead to tragedy and madness . . .

Rainer Werner Fassbinder's "Lola" 1982.

Lola the maneater and her garter belts which drive men crazy. . .

Marlene Dietrich in "The Blue Angel" 1930.

Clio Goldsmith.

Under-age or adult, some film stars, caught red-handed in their sexy underwear, plead not guilty.

Dustin Hoffman "The Graduate" 1967.

Jessica Lange "The Postman Always Rings Twice" 1981.

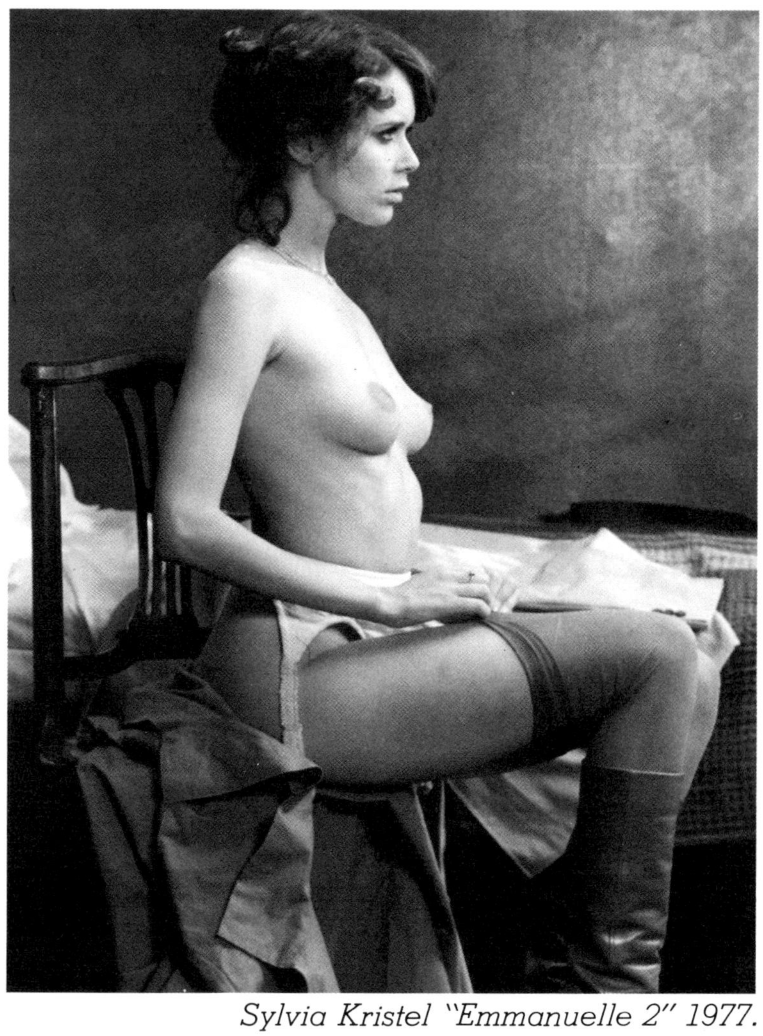

Sylvia Kristel "Emmanuelle 2" 1977.

Sydne Rome.

Jane Birkin "I Love You Me Neither" 1976.

Ursula Andress "Africa Express".

THE UNDERWEAR AFFAIR

As the century began, panting men would line up at bus stops and next to puddles to watch for the moment when a woman was forced to lift the hem of her dress a bit too high, and involuntarily show the bottoms of her long bloomers. One brief glimpse of an ankle was enough to spark the frustrated desires of these unfortunate, hot-blooded men who had only their fantasies to excite them. Over the years, though, sexuality evolved in due course. Women created a stir when they left those high, stiff-collared bodices behind; there were controversial cinematic stripteases; movie houses were showing half-naked actresses; and sunbathers adopted two-piece bathing suits to get a better tan at the beach, in spite of the uproar that style initially provoked. In brief, with each new scandal mentalities began to change, mores became more relaxed and society moved out of its puritanical phase, beginning a more permissive trend. Libidinal perverts, insatiable pornographers, jovial orgy enthusiasts, mad fetishists, methodical mate-swappers, bizarre maniacs, ribald voyeurs and sadomasochists were now able to come out of the closet. Everyone managed his own taboos and sexual fantasies, without having to answer to anyone else (except one's own libido).

While the average person discovered the accessible joys of sex, psychologists, sexologists, sociologists, and all the other "ists" were fascinated by the motivations, impulses, obsessions, and failures. They took extensive surveys crammed with indiscreet questions, conducted many experiments on those consenting humans; and published their findings in large books with explanations for their readers on the mechanisms of desire and the operatives of pleasure. Those who were dissatisfied with their sex lives could now be treated, like any other patient. But sexologists were not the only ones to take an interest in the sexual fantasies of the masses. Concept sellers, those who developed the ideas and finished products of their time, were quick to understand the advantages of marketing erotic impulses. In order to control the consumer, they learned how to manipulate them through the power of sex; "When I show you this, does it titillate or stimulate you?" They soon began to play on free associations, double-meanings, and putting thoughts in the backs of our heads . . .

Many precautions were necessary—after all, unbridled eroticism is a potentially dangerous force. When indiscriminately used, it could have disastrous consequences upon the image of a product's brand name. Meticulous marketing research goes into every advertising campaign, and whoever creates an image that will feed the public must carefully gauge the degree of sexual impact. Sometimes it is necessary to eliminate all traces of eroticism from a photograph, as effectively as would a Father of Decency, and especially when the publicity concerns children. At other times, it is necessary to inflate allusions to the point of outright provocation. The overall picture that the public will see must convey a precise message, sustained by a carefully studied atmosphere, according to its target. Depending on the campaign, you either get a shot of oxygen, the famous breath of fresh air, or the bouncy bottom.

If lingerie is being marketed, the advertisers walk on thin ice. This kind of product is tendentious, because its presentation must never discourage the eventual buyer. The girl being photographed is almost always half-naked (it is difficult to promote brassieres or briefs when other garments cover them up!), and the art director is counting on the youth and beauty of his/her model for aesthetic purposes; but the model must have a cer-

continued on page 74

tain asexual quality, for moral purposes.

After that, everything depends on the photograph: severe, with few accessories, the frames are unimaginative, and the poses are completely immobile. The photographers give the consumers strict, straight, and structured products that are impossible to misinterpret. Naughty thoughts could not lay with any greater ease against the mannequin's skin than panties would have under Marilyn's dresses . . . To be able to fantasize about a girdle or slip ad is a prodigious accomplishment, and occasionally, a neurotic one. There is little difference between a live model posing for a support bra and the wax-models that wear them in shop windows. One of the undergarment manufacturers went so far as to photograph its bra line on sculptured torsos. An interesting detail of these torso sculptures is that the smooth black busts have neither arms nor heads, and clearly display the reasoning behind their development: they are only display units, fillers, and foils. What must be admired are the insolent and audacious bras stuck on these works of art, like a sign of the times on a vestige of yesteryear.

Obviously, not every advertising campaign for lingerie follows the same, aseptic format. Some makers turn their backs, more or less openly, on this boring image, and give their products some soul. It would be impossible not to mention Dim, the French panty hose and lingerie maker whose catchy tune is immediately recognizable. Dim's promotional

continued on page 76

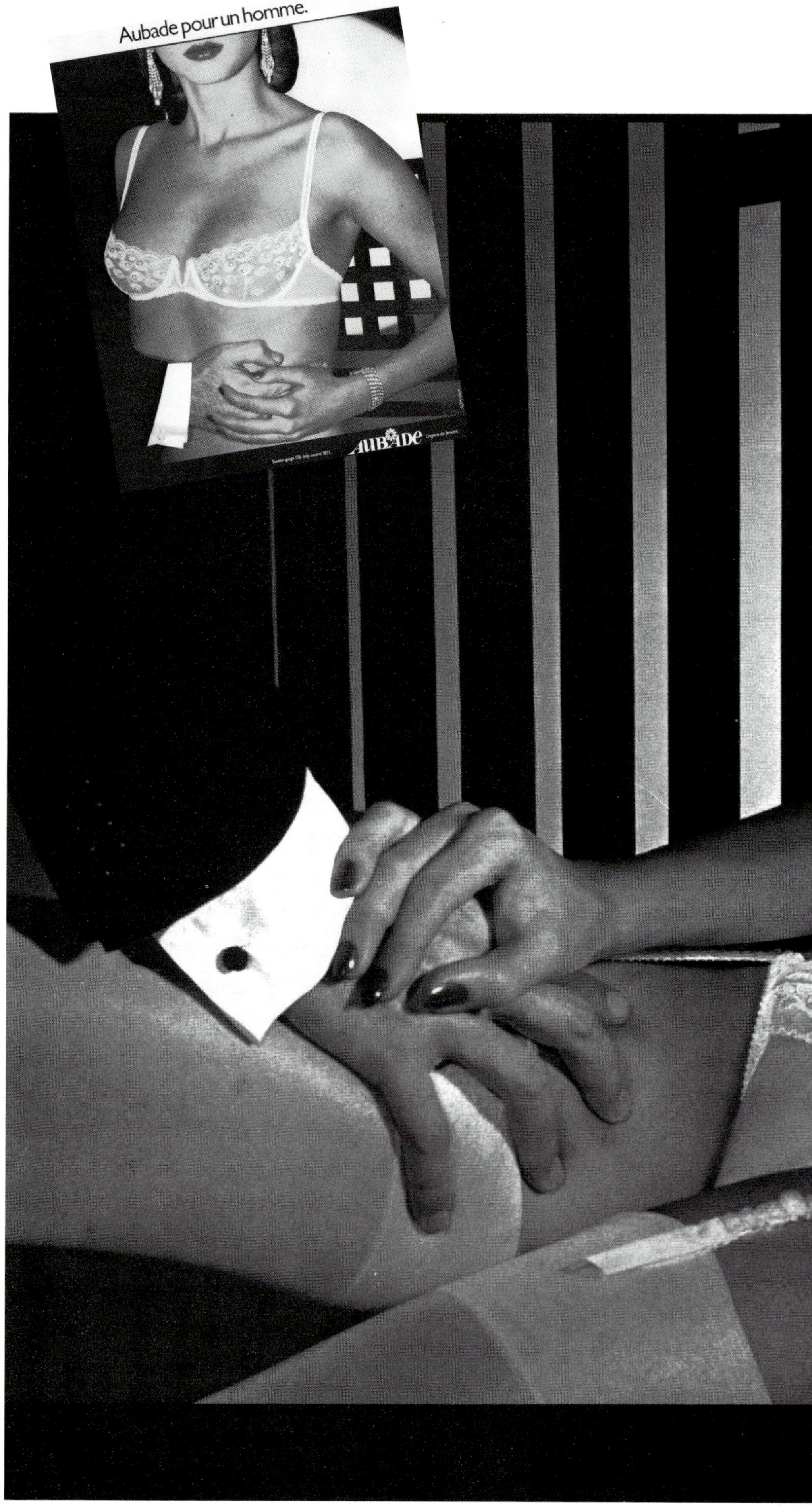

Ensemble : soutien-gorge 506 - slip porte-jarretelles 522 (ou slip assorti 514).
AUBADE
Lingerie

Dim gets dramatic

efforts are both imaginative and daring. Whether we are visually invited into a fashionable loft, an Asian colonial house, or an artist's studio, the Dim charm works, and we feast our eyes upon the fantasy. I wouldn't go so far as to say that the average viewer remembers the name of the particular style everytime, but he has definitely memorized the brand name, and that is really what counts: the posters on the wall are in charge of refreshing his memory.

Triumph brand underwear formulated a suggestive campaign on this theme. Soft photography and suave sensuality made it easy to look at. In the Rosy series, which combines chic, nonchalant, beautiful and curvaceous girls with white marble, a certain evening languor comes to mind, along with fantasies of an Italian holiday. Of course, the model is looking right into your eyes, as they do in all of today's stylish lingerie ads, but those pupils contain a certain look, which is infinitely more rare. She is near, distant and dreamy, yet available. And then there is the infamous Aubade lingerie campaign in France, conceived to provoke scandal. Something very rare happens in these lingerie ads: a man appears in the picture (the last striking antecedent was that of a young man rubbing his nose against a bra made by Dim). But this time the man doesn't appear sweet and nice like the Dim lover. He's a hard man, a macho man: you can tell by looking at his hand. In fact, his hand is the only thing you see. The hand is disembodied, but that makes it easier for a man who's looking at the ad to attach his own face and body to the hand that grasps the thigh, or the stomach, of the woman who has only a mouth as a means of identification (and don't tell me you can't make heads or tails of this). You might see it as Man and Woman in their best roles: the great Seduction Game. She has her hand on his, you don't know whether it is to discourage him ("I'm not the kind of woman you think I am"), or to keep it next to her body ("touch me again"). Audacious and deliberately provocative, unlike the Rosy or Triumph ads, this campaign gives underwear some of the erotic power it might have lost.

It is also interesting to note that articles of lingerie sometimes play leading roles in shoe ads. From the Eram-brand slip (woman searching through drawer), to the Carel-brand garter belt and panties (lying on a bed), underwear sells shoes. Could it be accidental or is it an artful coupling of distant yet friendly fetishes? It is difficult to say, but I would personally tend toward the latter interpretation, even without sufficient proof . . .

T'es Dim jusqu'au bout!
DIM
COLLANT · PANTYHOSE
Pointe et talon invisibles, maille veloutée, c'est le Doux Super-fin : soyez Dim jusqu'au bout des pieds !
DIM

Contrary to the passing fads of the modernized "retro" fashion, wherein the garment is picked off of the outdated rack of history and always looks a little out of place (because its life has already ended and it no longer corresponds to anything), the comeback of the undergarment is a very real, significant and fascinating phenomenon of society.

At the beginning of its career, underwear was but a stage in undressing, or in dressing. When a girl was caught in her underwear, it was as though she were naked; its function was a private one, concerning only the girl in question, or whoever else she might allow to be present; it intensified a precise moment of waiting, either for more clothes to be put on over it, or for a night of love. Nowadays, in movies and in commercial or fashion photography, underwear has a new function. It is no longer an intimate, secret, and personal affair. Hundreds of women have displayed their bodies in underclothes, and they never had the look of shame and surprise of women who have just been compromised. On the contrary. As if it were the most natural thing in the world, they were happy to walk about with the greatest calm. Thus, what they wore was rendered commonplace, simply by the way they wore it. Underwear became just another way of dressing, a full-fledged garment in its own right, recognized and respected as such. It had so often

continued on page 80

been displayed that everyone was familiar with its innumerable shapes and multiple uses. In addition to being self-sufficient, it no longer needed to be hidden. Everyone had studied it closely, and men were saying to themselves: so that's all underwear really is: a jumble of lingerie, wrapped around a body. In lifting the taboo, and explaining the magic, the image and the spell of underwear had been broken. Thanks to more liberal mores and to feminism, the garter belt was done away with. Only a handful of fanatics, prostitutes, transvestites and femmes fatales, for the most part, kept a nice collection of suggestive underwear in their closets. If a woman wore sexy underwear, she was undoubtedly a seductress, and ready to go to any lengths to turn a man on.

Little by little, frou-frou underwear became the symbol of absolute femininity, whether real or imagined, and perfectly adopted, with its well-kept secrets, its difficult access, and its promises of pleasure. And the very thing that made women want to banish underwear forever, that is to say the ambiguous, fetish-related role it played with the desires of men, brought back its positive image. Women wanted to please once again, and, when they felt good, to provoke desire.

As soon as they were given a choice, the act of putting on a fitted corselet was no longer a part of their dreadful, everyday confinement, but instead a kind of mischievous game of charm, to which gentlemen were quite sensitive. It has always been difficult to resist a woman who has worked so hard at destroying your self-control. Between the woman wearing sexy underwear and a man who looks at her runs a strong current of erotic complicity.

Underwear never lost its powers of persuasion, even during its short eclipse. On the contrary, it has improved with age, in public recognition and in the clarity of its intentions; it pleases me to please you, so I do all I can to, and everybody's happy.

Men had let the use of underwear abate without really reacting, first of all, because they did not necessarily feel comfortable facing women who were discovering their independence and feminism, and, secondly, because the image of underwear became too highly publicized and, therefore, lost a bit of its mystery. But the intimate and exciting ritual of the savory undergarment was quick to haunt thousands of frustrated nostalgics at night. Can it possibly be true that, somewhere, the female body continues to frighten more than a few gentlemen? Of course, specialized magazines and well documented films give them information on the enemy anatomy. And women no longer fear being naked in front of them. But all this is not enough to dispel the disturbing aspects of the body they must both possess and satisfy. It is easy to feel clumsy with a beautifully smooth and fleeting body on your hands; like the great unknown, it is ungraspable, unmalleable, and offers nothing substantial to hold on to for the anxious lover. He does not know where to begin to grasp this assemblage of zones with special, erogenous spots; meanwhile he must try to possess it, and not give up until he does. Underwear can be of great help to he who trips all over his desires, and feels—with horror—that his anxiety is not a very positive influence on the delicate mechanisms that control his physical impulses. And now

continued on page 86

he's trapped in a vicious circle: the more nervous he gets, the less assurance he projects, and with the subsequent loss of confidence, the more nervous he gets. By being the maestro in the great orchestra of suggestive underwear, he gains the invaluable security of a tangible grasp on this abstract body, and becomes a master of the game. He hides, or uncovers as he pleases, the parts that inspire him, and veils everything that might intimidate him; he frames the object of his desires, and gives a new and more intimate dimension to the entire ritual. Underwear is a garment, like any other, with reassuring and familiar connotations. The minute details of preparation, that could very well lead to other things, are indispensable stimulants for him, allowing him to have a satisfying rapport with the other's body. He knows where he's going, and thus feels like getting there.

There are as many male eyes set on female underwear as there are varied personalities. Some love to look at the tenuous outline of panties under skin-tight jeans, while naive girls sporting black bras under white shirts drive them especially mad. What turns some men on, turns others off, for instance those who only like invisible underwear, reserved for whoever has the pleasure of undressing the discreet seductress. That type of man prefers surprise-packets rather than exhibited charms. To unfasten a skirt, and discover the laces of a black garter belt, already provides strong visual stimulus for many men.

Black is a popular color for the sexual fantasies of many. But white also has many fans who feast on the color of innocence and purity as a powerful aphrodisiac. Others maintain that, no matter what anyone else says, panties must be pink, and if possible, made of breakable elastic, so that the numerous possibilities include that of dropping to their owner's an-

continued on page 94

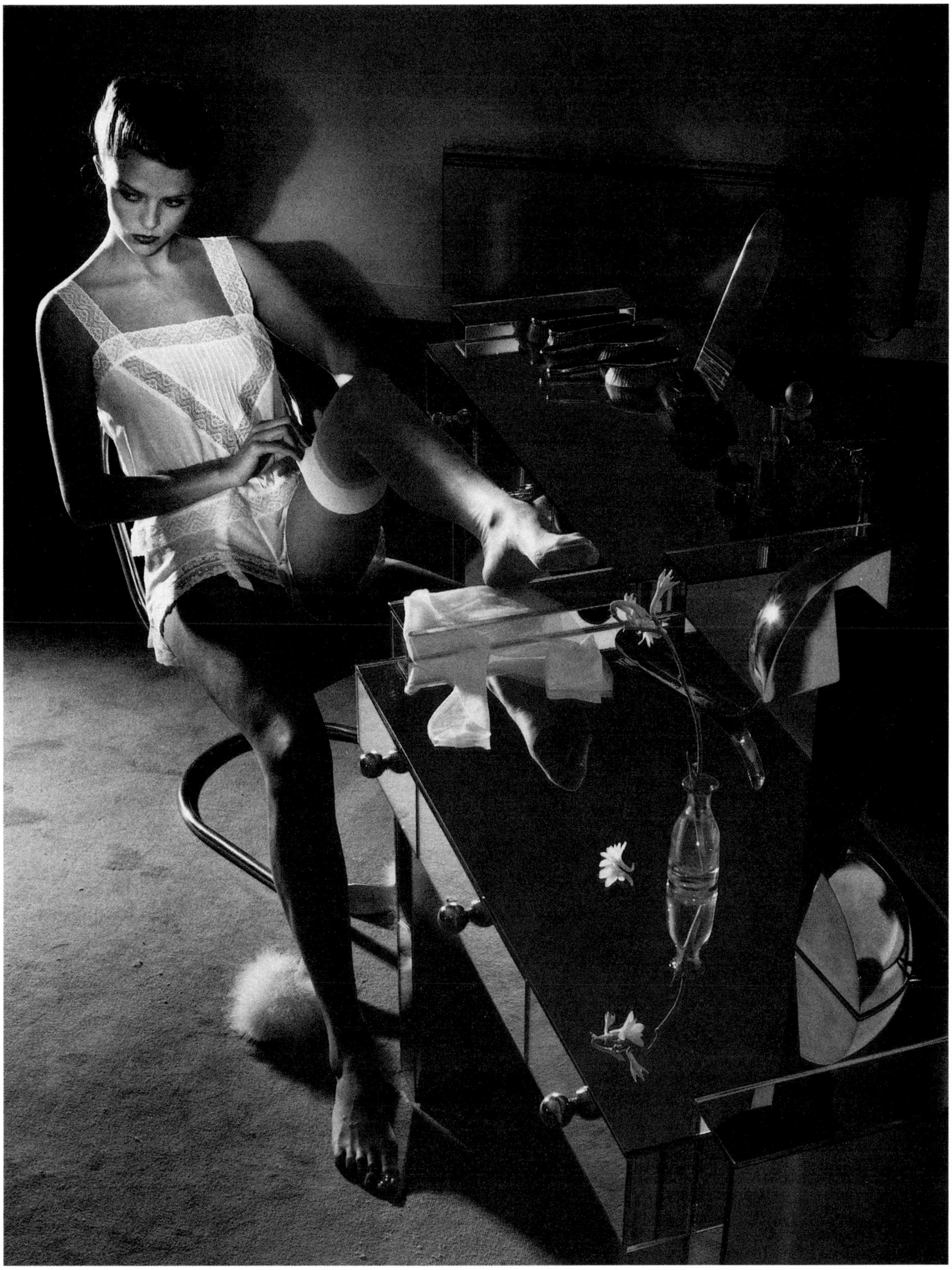

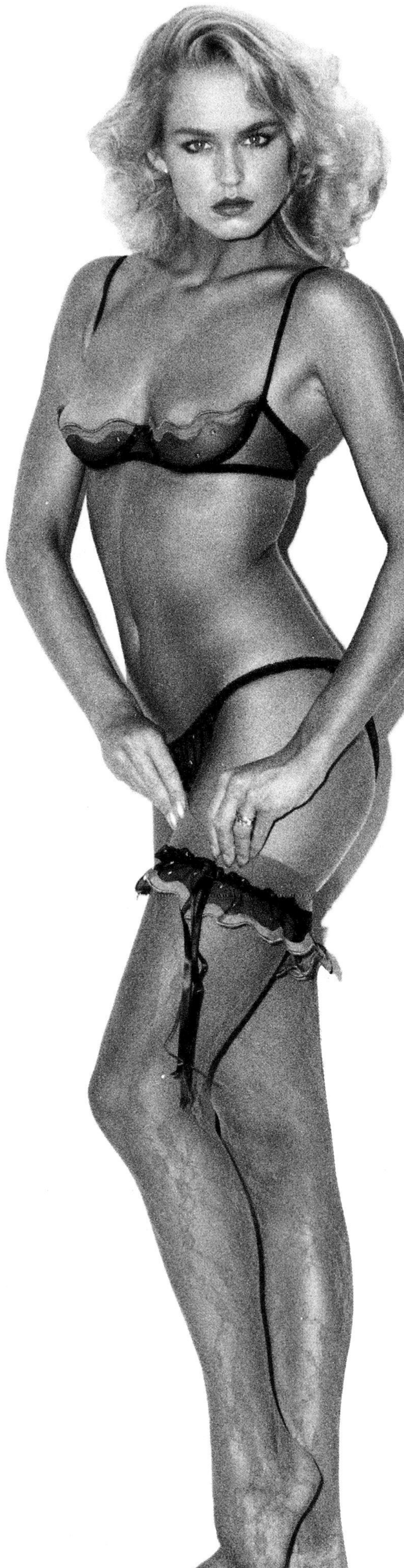

kles, to the great delight of any passers-by. That is, however, a very rare pleasure.

Men that adore a woman in stockings are particularly sensitive to the raspy noise legs make when they are being crossed. That soft, slinky sound immediately evokes visions of naked thighs encased in tight garters or stretched stocking suspenders, and a man's imagination will careen along those nylon-wrapped legs. To be able to caress the leg above the knee, and to have the intoxicating pleasure of going from the feel of the stocking texture to that of the soft, warm, and tender skin, would be, for him, the epitome of bliss. They are the avid followers of all these graceful stocking rituals, and they never grow weary of admiring the motions of a woman, whether she is putting her stockings on, or removing them.

Some men find those women who will go out with a run in their stockings an incredible provocation. This vertical and disturbing rip, so careless in appearance, lends an air of casualness that might turn to fantasies of casual, anonymous sex. Their sexual fantasies include the whispers of a stranger saying: "Take me, like an animal, darling, tear off all my clothes, lacerate my underwear, and let's make love like savages." It's the end of civilization, and we return to fighting over fire, and thus, over sex; it is the sweet-toothed savage, the screaming warrior, running after his dessert.

Innocent little lingerie doing a disappearing act.

Diversity in the shape and form of the fitted corselet are adored by an entirely different category of men. This lovely item can be long or short, with or without stocking suspenders, covering or uncovering the bosoms, but always very tight and shapely. In addition to being a positive element in the maintenance of the female bustline, fitted corselets also have the undeniable quality of always being sported, not by accident or out of necessity, but only for seductive purposes, by women with a taste for the unusual. When they wear them, women convey a certain idea of luxury and availability which intensifies their erotic impact on the discriminating man.

When one observes the way it looks, its causes and effects, one notices that the fitted corselet is a noble relative of the corset. For centuries, women have felt the need to imprison their busts in order to show them off, and men have always applauded this desire, since it simultaneously satisfied their own. Whether this type of underwear calls itself "fitted corselet, corselet, strapless brassiere or goes by the name of a waist-cincher, whether it opens in the front or in the back, who cares as long as the hips are unhindered, the waist thin, and the breasts provocative? The deviationists of the compressionist movement took its principle to the limit, and ended up with quite a spectac-

continued on page 98

ular perversion called "Bondage" (which the French call "Saucissonnage"). Usually wearing very limited black leather underwear, "Bondage" fans are tied up in the most uncomfortable positions by excited knot-lovers who like their ropes tight. At the end of the operation, the woman looks like a large sausage, all tied up with string. The tormentor can now whip or gently spank his helpless victim, exerting his ultimate control over the helpless, prone, and equally excited victim. The real object of the game is to dominate the body by compressing it as much as it can bear, in order to immobilize it completely, taking away all its freedom of shape and movement. The female body has lost its proper identity, and no longer can frighten, since it has been transformed into a string-tied roast, totally incapable of taking any kind of initiative, hardly able to breathe.

Most underwear fans, however, do not systematically resort to such means of oppression. On the contrary. Rather than constraining the body, they prefer more flattering underwear that tastefully caresses every contour. It's all a matter of pleasing the eye, and then the touch. Little loose camisoles with slipping straps, or tight-fitting silk body-suits that gently underline shapely curves without brutalizing them, and that close at the crotch with two miniscule snaps, can certainly arouse a gentleman's desire.

A curious and significant fact (and more widespread than one would believe), is that

continued on page 104

there are 100% heterosexual men who get their kicks out of wearing women's lovely frou-frou panties underneath their three-piece suits. It's their thing, and they enjoy the sensual pleasure (after all, why should the luxurious feeling of silk against the skin be reserved for women only?), as much as the erotic game (for the most part, they have stolen the panties from an unguarded drawer). No one in the street is able to guess what lies beneath those goodie-goodie trousers, and all of this is both amusing and exciting for them. But, as their mothers would say, what if they should have an accident? What a disgrace at the hospital!

These men like the feel of women's panties, and not only when they're about to have sex. Even as far afield as the rock and roll world, musician Frank Zappa probably does as well, because of that famous bedspread he owns, the one made of feminine panties sewn together, panties given to him by a love-crazed fan club. What do you dream about under such a bed-cover? Rock 'n' roll's Elvis Presley, who started off so well and ended up so badly, loved guns, food, cars, dope, and last but not least, women's panties.

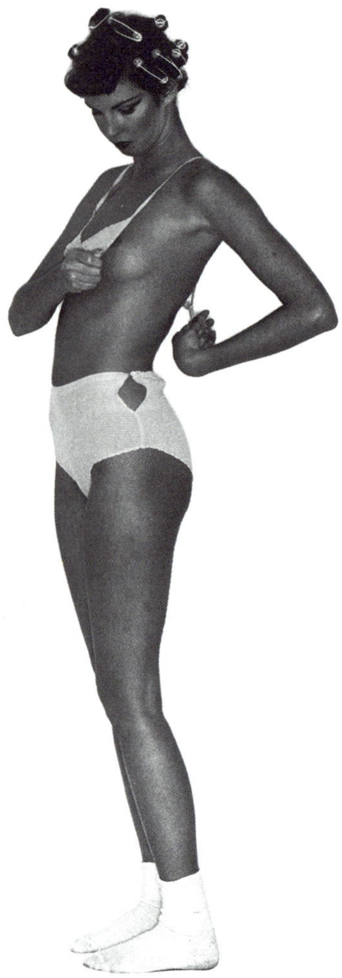

MILLER

Lately, the sexy underwear fad has hit the U.S.A., where more and more American housewives who used to organize neighborhood garage sales are scorning Tupperware conventions so that they may indulge in the exhilarating pleasures of the underwear trade. The organizer/initiator begins the sale, complete with models, and all the excited American women enjoy a display of fine and naughty lingerie for hours. They try it on, ask their buddies for advice, listen to every last detail of each others' experiences, speculate on their husbands' reactions; in brief, they have a good time while they wait for an even more delicious one. Those who have already tasted cupless bras, or slit panties, want more. The complete line of accessories are sold, left and right, and at the highest price, so great is the desire these women have to satisfy the whims of their breadwinning hubbies. The mistress of the apartment used for these "panty parties" has her choice of garment in return for her services, and certainly she will use it to its greatest potential.

We must also mention the Miss Underwear '83 Contest, organized by the manager of a lingerie chain; this brilliant idea has tripled her profits. Meanwhile, in Tokyo, there are undergarment bars, where waitresses wear only naughty underwear, and touching is allowed.

The pages of today's magazines, newspapers and mail-order catalogs are full of incredible styles of lingerie—some are

continued on page 116

much more open than closed, and most are tantalizing and very artistic. The only disadvantage of this special type of underwear lies not in the fact that it is called "Carla" or "Jasmine" but in that it is made of the most abominable material, synthetics that don't have the luxurious feel of natural fibers. Not to worry, though—if you're looking for silk, or even plain cotton, you can seek out Frederick's of Hollywood, Victoria's Secret, or the other specialists of fine lingerie who, because of our love for erotic, sensual underwear, have made mail-order and in-store lingerie sales reach into the millions of dollars every year. This is a far cry from the days when the mandatory dainties were sensible and handmade. There's no doubt about it: sexy underthings have a unique talent for keeping men and women around the world in absolute thrall.

THE UNDERWEAR AFFAIR

HISTORY 14

p. 14 Undies open and bottoms up

THE MOVIES 32

p. 38 Movie stars at your service
p. 63 Marilyn in fishnets
p. 65 Brigitte in a bustier: Bardot unveils her charms

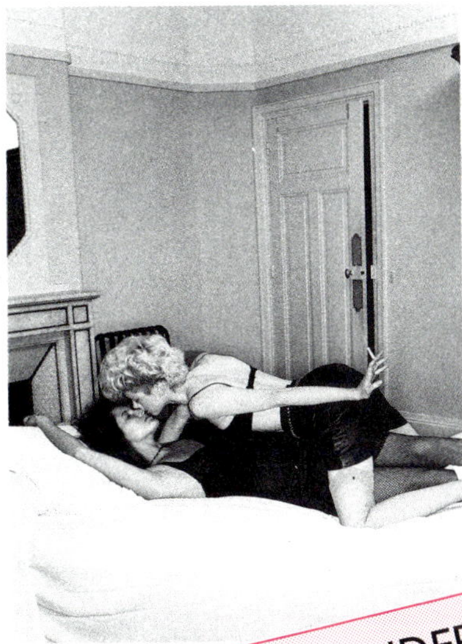

THE UNDERWEAR AFFAIR

71 ADVERTISING

p. 75 Advertising in Underwear

p. 76 Dim gets dramatic

84 HIGH FASHION

p. 13-71 Laurence Sackman / p. 73-112 Simon Bocanegra /
p. 78-79-84-85-87-88-89-110-111 Joe Gaffney /
p. 100-101-102-103 Denis Jobron /
p. 90-91-92-93-97-99-104 Claude Guillaumin /
p. 94-95 Reynaud-Art Pulsion / p. 96 Ingo Harney /
p. 98 Alberto Dell'Orto / p. 105 Jeff Dunas /
p. 106-107 Claus Wickrath / p. 108-109 Arthur Gordon /
p. 113-114-115-116-117-118-119-120 Didier Gaillard.

THANKS TO...

UNMENTIONABLES is especially grateful to:

SIMON BOCANEGRA - JEFF DUNAS - JOE GAFFNEY
DIDIER GAILLARD - CLAUDE GUILLAUMIN - ARTHUR GORDON
INGO HARNEY - KATHERIN HIBBS - DENIS JOBRON - JEAN DANIEL LORIEUX
REYNAUD/ART PULSIONS - LAWRENCE SACKMAN
CHRIS THOMSON - CLAUS WICKRATH

AUBADE - DIM - COSA NOSTRA - LEJABY
LES NUITS D'ÉLODIE - PUBLICIS
PRIMA - STAR DE PARIS

MURIEL BOSQUEY - MICHAELENE DONATI
SAMUEL FONTAYNE - STAN LEVY - ÉTIENNE MARIE
DOMINIQUE PINEL - ANNE PLETTENER
FRANKIE ROSENBEUM - SCG/JOURNAL A - WHERE
ARJA

CREDITS

SIMON BOCANEGRA p. 112 / JEFF DUNAS p. 105 / SAMUEL FONTAYNE p. 26, 27 /
JOE GAFFNEY p. 78, 79 - 84, 85 - 87 - 88, 89 - 110, 111 /
DIDIER GAILLARD p. 113 - 114, 115 - 116, 117 - 118, 119 - 120 /
CLAUDE GUILLAUMIN p. 90, 91 - 92, 93 - 97 - 99 - 104 / ARTHUR GORDON p. 108, 109 /
INGO HARNEY p. 96 / DENIS JOBRON p. 82, 83 / JEAN DANIEL LORIEUX p. 69 /
ALBERTO DELL'ORTO p. 98 / REYNAUD/ART PULSIONS p. 94, 95 /
LAWRENCE SACKMAN, Art Direction and Concept: STAN LEVY,
Models: BEATRICE and SUZANNE from the FAM agency p. 13 - 71 /
CHRIS THOMSON p. 30 - 31 / CLAUS WICKRATH p. 106 - 107.

COLLECTION RAYMOND BOYER
p. 9 - 10 - 23 - 28 - 33 - 35 - 38 - 42, 42 - 44, 45 - 46 - 56 - 62, 63 - 64 - 65 /
CHRISTOPHE L. p. 8 - 16, 17 - 32, 33 - 47 - 48 - 51 - 62 - 67 - 68, 69 /
COLLECTION PATRICE ENARD p. 18, 19 - 34 - 39 - 49 - 50, 51 - 54, 55 - 62 - 68 /
ESQUIRE MAGAZINE/NOV. 1943 p. 29 / GAMMA/PHOTO : ATLAN p. 69 /
GAMMA/PHOTO : CLAUDE AZOULAY p. 66 / INTER PRESS p. 21 /
ALAIN PELE p. 33 - 39 - 48 - 51 - 56 /
STARS FILMS
p. 7 - 14, 15 - 16, 17 - 23 - 32 - 36, 37 - 39 - 40, 41 - 49 - 50 - 53 - 55 - 57 - 64 - 66 - 68 /
UNITED PRESS PHOTOS p. 49 / WARNER BROS PICTURES p. 34, 35.